Psalms Now

Psalms Now

Paraphrased for Today

Isobel de Gruchy

RESOURCE *Publications* · Eugene, Oregon

PSALMS NOW
Paraphrased for Today

Copyright © 2022 Isobel de Gruchy. All rights reserved. Except for brief quotations in critical publications or reviews, no part of this book may be reproduced in any manner without prior written permission from the publisher. Write: Permissions, Wipf and Stock Publishers, 199 W. 8th Ave., Suite 3, Eugene, OR 97401.

Resource Publications
An Imprint of Wipf and Stock Publishers
199 W. 8th Ave., Suite 3
Eugene, OR 97401

www.wipfandstock.com

PAPERBACK ISBN: 978-1-6667-3704-2
HARDCOVER ISBN: 978-1-6667-9610-0
EBOOK ISBN: 978-1-6667-9611-7

AUGUST 1, 2022 8:52 AM

Contents

Acknowledgements | vii

Introduction | ix

THE PSALMS

   Psalm 1 – 150 | 1

Glossary | 225

Bibliography | 231

Acknowledgements

To John, my husband, I give special thanks. He was the one who encouraged me to publish my paraphrased psalms. He has guided me at all times in the process, read, and reread what I wrote, and explained the mysteries of publishing to me. Special thanks also to my sister, Elsie Steel, who cast her expert eye over the full manuscript and made valuable suggestions. To Anton, my son, thanks for always being there to answer questions about, and patiently sort out, computer problems. Also, thanks to Esther, my daughter-in-law for her help and care. My thanks also go to:

The monks of St Benedict's Priory, now situated next-door to us in the Volmoed Retreat and Conference Centre, who allowed me to keep books out of their library for an inordinately long time.

Reinette Swarts and Ann van Schalkwyk who kept the house from falling into chaos while I worked with words.

My other friends on Volmoed who supported me.

Friends from further afield who read excerpts and offered welcome encouragement.

To these and others who, unbeknown to themselves, have given me insights and helped develop any of my skills which have contributed to this enterprise,

And to all at Resource Publishing who have contributed to the bringing into being of this book.

And I add with the psalmist, "Give thanks to the Lord, for God is good."

Introduction

What Is the Book of Psalms?

Nestled in the Old Testament, between the history of Israel and the prophets, is a book of songs, prayers, hymns, and sayings called *The Psalms*. It has always played a central role in the life of Jewish people, and the Christian church from its beginning has revered it as well. It is still read today by Christian and Jew in their personal lives, and chanted, sung, and prayed by communities in their worship. It has been translated into hundreds of languages, but for 350 years there was only one version in English which was widely known and loved, the King James or Authorised Version. This was the only one I knew growing up. And I confess that I never had much love for the psalms. I struggled to understand them and disagreed with some of their content.

Modern translations did make the psalms easier to understand, but I could still not respond to them with much enthusiasm. Language is one thing, but content another, and not so easy to change. The psalms were full of people with enemies, wicked people who were always, for no reason it seemed, against the psalm-writer, self-righteous people, and an angry God. I was not alone in thinking this. Of course, there were those gems like the 23rd Psalm, "The Lord is my shepherd", which were known or at least recognised by most of the English-speaking world. This is sadly no longer the case. As a Christian I would wonder why the psalms were of any value, with their pre-Christian response to violence with more violence, and their moral code of "Do good and you will prosper. Do evil and you will suffer" and "Curse your enemies." This book is a result of trying to find out.

Introduction

Who Wrote the Psalms?

Many of the psalms have a title, "a psalm of David", but there is no historical evidence to support David as the author. Scholars have found that the titles were added much later than the psalms were composed. Most of the psalms were passed on orally at first and one version only written down later. They have changed in other ways as well as over the years adaptations and copying resulted in differences. Scholars admit they still do not know who wrote any individual psalm or exactly what event or situation inspired the words. No-one knows who Aseph, Ethan, Heynan, who are named in some titles, were. I have not used these titles, but instead given a descriptive sentence, in order to help identify each psalm.

When Were the Psalms Written?

The psalms were composed at different times. Robert Alter in *The Book of Psalms*, says that many of the psalms come from the Near Eastern world of the late Bronze Age. (1800–1200 BCE) so they are quite alien to us and our world. Early in the twentieth century hundreds of clay tablets were unearthed in a place called Ras Shamra, near the ancient town of Ugarit, in present-day Syria. The writing on them has been deciphered, and the language found to be similar to Biblical Hebrew. The poetry on some bore some resemblance to the psalms which has helped scholars come to a greater understanding of the language and meaning of the psalms, and to date some of them. Some could go as far back as David, but more likely to the time of Solomon, (996 BCE) and some to after the exile, in mid-sixth century BCE. Even so it is not possible to date any of them precisely, except to say that they were composed over many centuries.

What Kind of Psalms Are There?

The psalms according to their content, fall into two main divisions: those that are by an individual, either asking God for help, or thanking and praising God; and those that are communal. These are prayed by the nation pleading for help at times of great need or giving thanks and praise after a battle has been won. Some psalms exhort the reader to live an exemplary life while others tell the history of the nation. Many emphasise the basic reason for good behaviour, which is to avoid punishment and receive the

Introduction

reward of God's approval. Illness is one of the ways in which punishment comes. There are also the Royal Psalms, written to praise a king, celebrate a royal wedding, or a coronation.

The psalms are not arranged in any obvious order. They have been traditionally divided into five groupings, or "books". Some scholars say that these are not according to themes and that we do not know when this was done, nor who did it. It is also a later and artificial addition. There are others who see some pattern in the arrangement. One of the books, Book II, (Psalms 42 – 72) has a more distinguishing feature. It uses only Elohim (which is translated *God*), as the name for God: In the Bible the name for God is either Yahweh (translated *The Lord*) or Elohim. (translated *God*) (see the Glossary)

How Do We Relate to the Psalms?

As we have seen, the psalmist's understanding of the way in which his world is ordered and how he and his contemporaries conduct their everyday affairs is so very different from ours. This makes it difficult to relate to them. And those of us who are Christians have other objections which lead us to question why the psalms are so important. The answer may just lie in the fact that what they do convey is an image of human attitudes and behaviour which, despite all the differences, mirrors our own, in its suffering, illness, violence, jealousies, being lost and lonely, betrayed and in despair, looking for answers, and looking for God. We see ourselves in these prayers and poems.

What This Book Is and Is Not

My attitude towards *The Psalms,* given all the above, was still largely negative. This worried me and, in an attempt to change this, I thought of trying to get behind the external wrappings of each psalm and find its deeper meaning. I felt I could do this by putting its sentiments into my own words, or how I imagine the original writer's sentiments might have been. That is, I could paraphrase each psalm to try and uncover its intention – basically a twenty/twenty-first century white African woman, starting off as a scientist, and becoming later a poet and artist, trying to find out what an Israelite male of about 3000 years ago meant when he composed a prayer to God.

Introduction

I also intended to put my version into the English of today which I did over the ensuing months. The result is not altogether in today's language. That language is multiple – each community in the English-speaking world has their own way of expressing things. The language of rural England is different from the street lingo of New York, that of an old Kenyan man from a young adult in Hong Kong. I hope however that my words would say something to them, should they come across this book. I speak to those who want something current, but not clever and "trendy". I hope that my words have gravitas without being ponderous or obscure. I have tried to get to the essence of what the writer of the psalm is saying using everyday words but also, inevitably some "religious" language. I trust that the Holy Spirit has provided the necessary inspiration and guidance.

When I showed some of my renderings to family and friends, they encouraged me to work further on them and publish them, which I have done. This book is the result. As I have said, it is not a translation of the psalms. This is a paraphrase, and a fairly loose one at that.

This is also not primarily a scholarly work – I did not use any commentaries initially, nor do I know any Hebrew, except for a few words. I originally used the King James Version with a few other translations as back up. I revised the work using other translations as well as the books that I have listed in the Bibliography. Although not a scholarly work, the resulting paraphrases are also not un-scholarly. Along with the other resources I used, I have valued and called upon the understanding I have accumulated from my formal and informal study of the Scriptures over many years.

What Makes This Book Different and Worth Reading?

First of all, I am a woman, and there are very few women authors of books on the Psalms. I am however a woman over the allotted "two score years and ten" given to us in the psalms. (Ps 90:10) I grew up before feminists improved our lot, although I am fully aware of the way women's voices have been ignored. My paraphrases are gender-neutral when referring to people. When referring to God, although I no longer think of God in terms of an old white male, I think the English language is made clumsy and awkward if we avoid using the pronouns *he* or *his* altogether and substitute them each time with the words *God* or *Lord*, even if we rework the sentence. As a poet I feel then that the rhythm and natural flow of the language is lost.

Introduction

Nevertheless, I use as much inclusive language as I can, and I do bring a woman's perceptions and sensitivity to the resulting poems with an older woman's wisdom and wealth of experience. I discuss this also below in Problem Words and Concepts.

I am white, but see myself as a white African, looking at life through broader eyes than those of someone only aware of the Northern Hemisphere and the First World. The outlook from Africa, and South Africa in particular, surely makes this different from other renderings of the Psalms.

I do have some biblical scholarship in my background, having done some formal university courses, as well as auditing other courses on spirituality and running church bible studies for many years.

I have a scientific background. My first love was Mathematics which I studied together with Botany at university. I have the scientist's insistence on clear reasoning which leads to making logical decisions. This also means that I have difficulty with the worldview expressed in the Psalms. (For more detail, see the Glossary.) The question is if and how one can put concepts such as the above into the thought forms and language of today. I decided in the end not to alter any too drastically. That would be recomposing the psalms, not paraphrasing them. This means that questionable science is viewed as metaphor.

I am also a poet. I try to be both rhythmical and poetic. I have mostly stuck to the "parallelism" of the original, where it is found. My first question has been, "How would we say this today?" and I try to get at the meaning and not the exact words. I then ask a second question, "How can this be said rhythmically, and even memorably?" I hope I have done that when called for.

I am a great admirer of Julian of Norwich (1342 – c1414), the fourteenth century English mystic. I have steeped myself for over 30 years in her writings and have written books, meditations and poetry based on them. I bring her outlook, and maybe a few of her phrases, to these paraphrases. It is her writings that have been pivotal in helping me see how relevant the psalms are. I take this up again later.

Finally, I add to the other aspects that I bring to this volume the fact that I was diagnosed with Parkinson's Disease nineteen years ago. It is always there with me, sometimes in the forefront, sometimes under the control of modern medicines. I have been struggling to live creatively with it since diagnosis.

Introduction
Problem Words and Concepts

The question arises as to how to deal with words that are no longer in common usage. There are objects that are out of date, such as weapons and armoury (bows and arrows, swords,) musical instruments, (zither, lyre) perfumes, (cassia, myrrh) etc. I have largely kept the old words and if necessary, explained them in the Glossary. Where possible I have brought words and figures of speech up to date.

Some concepts have become outdated even since the nineteen-seventies. We do not generally talk about "sinners", "the wicked", or "the righteous" these days. Both the words, and also the concepts they express, are no longer generally understood as they were, but substitute words are not always adequate. I have used the Glossary to explain how I have approached this.

Then there is the thorny issue of the gender of God, which I raised above. Do I drop all use of male pronouns for God? Or do I leave the words and concepts as they are, as with the other topics above? I try to balance the use of inclusive words with the need to keep rhythm and ease of flow. For myself, hearing masculine pronouns for God no longer bothers me as much as it did. I translate the image of a male God in my mind into how I personally image God. I do the same for example, in Psalm 21.12, with the God who aims arrows at the enemy with a bow. I don't see God doing that, so do I substitute the bow with a gun? Do I change each male pronoun into the words God or the Lord? Reading a string of Gods and God's in one sentence bothers me more. These are real issues that I wrestled with. There are also other images I disagree with, e.g. the Psalmist saying that God directly causes storms, (Ps 18:9–14) another that he created us directly. (Ps 33: 9,15) I have not dropped such images belonging to a pre-scientific era but regard them as metaphor. I have endeavored to use inclusive language for God as much as possible, but not exclusively.

How Julian of Norwich Helped Change My Mind

What Julian of Norwich thought about the Psalms I do not know. I have not found any reference to them in her writings, but I am sure she knew them well. However, several of her key concepts are directly opposed to the attitudes displayed in the psalms. For example. Julian "can see no anger in God", (*Showings*, chapter 46) and I agree. The same applies to God acting

Introduction

in any violent way towards people. God's love is portrayed as conditional in the psalms, but all-embracing in Julian's writings.

Then I began to see more and more similarities in their views. The psalmists proclaim again and again, that everything will turn out just fine for the good people, and God will destroy the wicked, even though this is not apparent. It dawned on me that as a Christian, it is not obvious that Jesus won a decisive victory on the cross – it still looks as though evil rules the world. I also have to take this on faith. Julian of Norwich also accepted in faith that "All shall be well, and all shall be well, and all manner of thing shall be well" (*Showings*, chapter 27) even though it was not. Are these any different?

They had the same goals. Both wanted God to be glorified and to be known throughout the world. Both proclaimed God as the creator of all that is, and the one in charge. God cares for each person and is the one who looks after and keeps safe each and everyone. One can only be happy if one is walking in the way of the Lord, although this is expressed differently by them and by us, but clearly we all have the same goals.

Conclusion

As this began to dawn on me, I began to find pearls of great price, and buried treasures, in the psalms. As Julian reaches across the centuries to speak to us today when one spends time and effort to delve into her writings, so I found do the psalms. May this book help to make the digging and delving easier. I want to add to this the invitation that, as you use the psalms in this book in your own or the church's worship, you are free to adapt any of these versions to make them speak into your own situation. Please just acknowledge their source. May your purpose be the same as theirs. Both the psalms and Julian have the same overarching message. God who created all that is, rules over it all, and true happiness can be found only in God. The meaning of everything is love, and God is love.

This stands out in psalm after psalm, to which I add, Hallelujah! Praise the Lord!

Isobel de Gruchy
31 March 2022
Volmoed

BOOK I

Psalms 1–41

Psalm 1

Happiness comes from taking delight in God's Law

1   Happy are those who do not walk along the path of wrongdoers,
or stand together with nonbelievers,
nor do they sit with those who pour scorn on believers.

2   They constantly have the law of the Lord in mind,
reciting it with great delight.

3   Each one will be like a tree,
planted on the banks of a flowing stream.
Its leaves never wither,
and it produces fruit in due season.
So too will all their undertakings prosper.

4   Nonbelievers, on the other hand,
are as unsubstantial as leaves blown before the wind.

5   At judgement time these nonbelievers
will not have a leg to stand on,
nor will sinners in the gatherings of the just.

6   Their way leads to destruction.
But God knows who the righteous are,
and shows them his way.

Psalm 2

A warning to earth's rulers (one of the oldest of the psalms)

1	Why do the nations become agitated and hatch their futile plans?
2	Why do their kings and rulers gather to plot against the Lord and the one anointed?
3	They say, "We will end our bondage, break our chains apart."
4	In reality it is the God above who laughs at them in derision.
5	But God is also angry, and declares,
6, 7	"I have set my king in Zion, and say to him,"—so listen, everyone— "You are my son, from the day I conceived you.
8	You have only to ask, and I will give you all the earth to possess, and all the nonbelievers to rule.
9	You will break them into pieces like a potter's flawed vessel, like a person being disciplined with a rod of iron."
10	So show some sense, you kings, look with intelligence and be wise, you princes.
11	Acknowledge the Lord with reverence, and rejoice in God with deference.
12	Embrace God's son before he gets angry— for he can flare up in an instant. Those who put their trust in God will be blessed indeed.

Psalm 3

Even with thousands against me I will not be afraid

1. Lord, I have so many enemies,
   so many who are against me.

2. They tell me that you will not help me.

3. But Lord, the glorious one,
   you hold my head up high and shield me.

4. Whenever I cry out to you,
   you answer me from your holy mountain.

5. I go to sleep knowing the Lord is there,
   looking after me.

6. No matter how many thousands are circling me about,
   I will not be afraid.

7. O Lord,
   Rise up and deliver me from them all.
   Give them what they deserve.

8. The Lord is the one who delivers us,
   and blesses the people of God.

Psalm 4

Those who trust in God are assured of help and of happiness

1. O God, on the side of the righteous,
   hear me when I call to you.*
   You answered me previously when I was in trouble,
   answer me now in your mercy.

* This phrase, variously rendered as:
When I call out, answer me,
Answer me when I call, O God,
or Hear me when I call to you.
is usually the formula for opening a psalm of supplication.

Psalm 5

2   O people, how long are you
    going to besmirch God's glory?
    How long lust after that which has no meaning
    and which belittles you?

3   Just know that the Lord has chosen to embrace
    those who are faithful.
    God will hear me when I call.

4   Stand before God in awe,
    without any sin in your heart.
    Be still, turn to God before you sleep,
    and look deeply into your own heart.

5   Offer to God the sacrifice
    of a life of just actions,
    and trust in the Lord.

6   Many are searching for someone
    who can show them the right way.
    Lord, smile on us with your light
    and be our guide.

7   You have filled my heart with a greater joy
    than when the harvest of grain and wine
    topped all before it.

8   When I go to bed at night, I will sleep in peace,
    for you, O God, have made me unafraid.

Psalm 5

*A plea to God to protect the righteous and those who honor God,
and to destroy their enemies*

1   Lord, give your ear to my words,
    your attention to my sighing.

2   My God and my King, listen to me
    when I cry for help.

3	In the morning I plead my case before you and wait. In the morning you hear my voice.
4–6	You are a God who takes no pleasure in wickedness— you allow no evil anywhere near you. The debauched cannot come into your presence. You do not tolerate those who do wrong. You abhor those who are blood-thirsty and spread lies and deceit. You will put an end to them all.
7	But, through your mercy, I may come into your holy temple to honor you, and enter your house in reverent awe of you.
8	Through the abundance of your enduring love, and because of my enemies, lead me on the straight path of right-doing. Show me the way.
9	For they flatter you, God, with their tongues, while uttering not one true word, because destruction comes from their hearts, and their throats are like open graves.
10	O God, may they declare their own guilt, and fall by their own counsel. Their sins are many because they have rejected your way.
11, 12	But let those who seek refuge in you rejoice. Let them sing for joy. Shield them with your protecting arm so that those who love your name may exult in you, for your favor and blessing cover the righteous like a shield.

Psalm 6

A plea for healing while suffering deeply

1. O Lord, if I have made you angry,
do not discipline me
or give me a dressing down.

2. Be gracious and listen to me,
for I am falling apart.
Heal me, for I am wracked with pain,
right through to my bones.

3. My soul itself is in anguish.
Where are you, God?
When will you come?

4. Turn to me, O Lord, and deliver me.
Save my life, in keeping with your steadfast love.

5. For how can I praise you,
or give you honor, from among the dead?

6. I am constantly overwhelmed by tears and groans.

7. At night they drench my bedclothes,
and by day they curtain my eyes.

8. Be gone now, all evildoers,
for the Lord has heard my cries.

9. He has acknowledged my weeping,
and accepted my prayers.

10. My enemies will soon be the ones
filled with terror—
they will suddenly be put to shame,
and be forced into retreat.

Psalm 7

A plea to God, the righteous judge, for help against the enemy

1,2   O Lord, my God, I take refuge in you.
        Save me! For those chasing me
        want to drag me off and tear me apart,
        as a lion does its prey.
        They will do so unless you protect me.

3   But Lord, if I am at fault,
      if I am the one in the wrong,

4   The one causing hurt to my friends,
      or destroying the enemy without cause,

5   Then it is right that I be caught by the enemy,
      and trampled to the ground,
      my honor biting the dust.

6   Arise, Lord, in your anger.
      Rouse yourself against the fury of my enemies.
      Wake up and set up the courts of judgement.

7   Call an assembly of the people together
      with you as Chief Justice.

8   Judge all the people.
      Judge me according to my right actions,
      according to my integrity.

9   Judge the wicked and stop their evil.
      But let the righteous stand firm,
      after you test both their minds and hearts,
      O Righteous Judge.

10   God shields me from evil,
       and saves all those who are good
       through and through.

11   God is a righteous judge
       who condemns those who do wrong.

PSALM 8

12-14* As a fighter God readies his weapons
against those who do not repent
and turn away from doing wrong,
against those who conceive evil,
those who are pregnant with conceit
and give birth to lies.

15 They dig a pit—let them fall into it themselves.

16 May their conceits rebound on their own heads
and their violence turn on them.

17 I will give thanks to God
for his righteousness
and sing praises to our Lord,
to the God above all others.

PSALM 8

Meditation on creation and our place in it

1 O Lord, our God!
How majestic is your name throughout the world!
Your glory, which stretches far beyond the heavens,
is praised from the mouths of infants and toddlers.

2 You built a fortress for your dwelling,
having silenced the enemy and the avenger.

3 When I gaze out
into the vastness of space,
with its stars and moons
all fashioned by your fingers,

4 I marvel, "What are we humans in your eyes?
We mortals who are so insignificant?"

---

* Verses 12,13—the exact translations of these verses depict God as a warrior who sharpens his sword and pulls taught his bow, aiming his arrows at those who do evil. Then he lets his arrows fly at those who do not repent. I have left out details such as this which show God using such violence, here and elsewhere.

5   Yet you have ranked us
just below any other gods there may be,
and crowned us with honor and power.

6   You have given us authority over all that you made,
putting all of it into our keeping.

7   From sheep and cattle to animals that roam wild,

8   From the birds of the air to the fish in the sea,
and other creatures who move along the currents of the sea.

9   O Lord, our God!
How majestic is your name throughout the world!

Psalm 9*

God judges rightly and rules justly

1   With all my heart I will give thanks to you, O Lord.
I will tell others of your wonderful deeds.

2   I will rejoice and exult in you.
I will praise you in song, O Lord above all.

3   My enemies turned back in defeat.
They stumbled and fell headlong,
because you were there.

4   For you were the judge on high,
and you judged rightly,
in favor of my just cause.

5   You rebuked the nations in the wrong,
and erased them from the books.

6   Their cities lie in ruins—
their very names have vanished,
and all memory of them is wiped out.

---

* Scholars have found the available texts of Psalm 9 difficult to decipher, both in tense and meaning. There is evidence it formed an acrostic poem together with Psalm 10.

Psalm 9

7 But you, Lord, are on your throne forever,
your seat of judgement.

8 You judge the world without bias,
the peoples straight and true.

9 O Lord, you are a fortress for the oppressed,
and a secure haven when trouble comes.

10 Those who know you trust you.
You do not abandon those who look to you for help.

11 Sing praises to the Lord who lives in Zion!
Tell everyone of God's deeds.

12 For God cares for those who have shed their blood,
and does not forget the cry of the afflicted.

13 Be gracious to me, O Lord.
See how I am made to suffer by those who hate me.
You can lift me up from the gates of death,

14 And set me at the gates of Zion,
where I can praise you
and rejoice in your deliverance.

15 The nations have themselves sunk
into the pit that they dug,
and caught their feet
in the net that they set up.

16 For you, Lord, are known by your justice,
the wicked by being snared in their own traps.

17 The wicked will end up in Sheol
as will all the nations that reject God.

18 The poor and those who are in great need,
will not always be the ones to die,
hopeless and forgotten.

19 Stir yourself, O God, do not let mere mortals
get the better of you.
Rather be the one to judge them.

20 Put the fear of God in them,
and show them that they are but mortal.

Psalm 10[*]

*A grim picture of the wicked who think there is no God,
and a plea to God to deal with them because he sees them all*

1. O Lord, why do you stand aloof?
   Why hide yourself in times of trouble?

2. The wicked in their arrogance persecute the poor—
   let them be caught in their own schemes.

3. The evildoers boast of their desires.
   The greedy curse and renounce the Lord.

4. In their pride, they do not even believe there is a God,
   or, if God exists, there is no place for him in their lives.

5. God, your judgements are not even noticed by them.
   They scoff at those made against them.

6. They think that they are forever immune from adversity—
   that they will always stand unharmed.

7. Their mouths spit out cursing, deceit, and falsehoods,
   and their tongues form evil and mischief.

8. They ambush their prey in town and village,
   and murder the innocent in secret.

9. Like a lion stalking its prey,
   their eyes follow the weak.
   They crouch down ready to pounce,
   dragging the poor victim to their den.

10. And the helpless fall into their clutches,
    felled by their might.

11. They think all the time, "God does not care.
    If he is there, he takes no notice."

13. Why do the evildoers renounce God
    and think he will not call them to account?

12. Rise up, O Lord, do not forget the oppressed.
    Raise your hand to help.

---

[*] Psalm 10 is thought to have been part of an acrostic poem together with Psalm 9.

14	In very truth you do see it all— you take note of every trouble and grief we suffer, in order to take it in hand. You have helped the orphan and the helpless who commit themselves to you.
15	Break the strength of those who are bent on wickedness. Search out evil till there is no more to be found.
16	For Lord, you are king for ever and ever. All nonbelievers shall perish from your land.
17, 18	You do listen to the desire of the weak. You will strengthen their hearts as you listen, so that terror does not strike them again, and justice is done to the orphan and the oppressed.

Psalm 11

The fate of the righteous and the wicked, under God, the just judge

1	It is in the Lord that I take refuge. How can you say to me, "Flee like a bird to the mountains"?
2	For look! The wicked already have their weapons at the ready, to shoot at the upright in heart, under cover of darkness.
3	If the foundations are destroyed what can the just person do?
4	The Lord is in his holy temple. His throne is in heaven, but his gaze is on all people— his look examines them.
5	The Lord tests the just and the evildoer alike. He hates those who pursue evil

6	He will pour out coals of fire and sulphur on them with a scorching wind.
7	For the Lord is a righteous God. He loves the just and the good they do. They are the ones who will see him face to face.

Psalm 12

Though the godly are few, God is on their side

1	Help! O Lord! For the godly are no more— the faithful have vanished, along with trust between people.
2	Those left utter lies and flattery to each other, with duplicity of heart.
4	Their tongues make great boasts. They claim to be masters of their own words.
3	May God cut these out of them.
5	Because they victimize the poor and terrify the needy with their threats, the Lord promises, "I will rise up and place them in safety".
6	God's promises are as pure as silver seven times refined.
7, 8	We know that you, O God, will protect us and guard us from this evil generation, for as long as vileness is exalted among humankind, and wickedness freely struts about.

Psalm 13

After pleading and waiting, God came to the rescue.

1   O God, how long will you go on forgetting me?
    How long will you turn your back on me?

2   How long must I bear sorrow in my heart day and night?
    How long let my enemy think they have won?

3   Give me an answer, O God,
    Cast a ray of light on me or I will die.

4   My enemy will claim victory
    and those opposed to me will celebrate.
    Darkness and despair will win the day.

5   But you were there for me.
    Because I kept on trusting in your constant love,
    now I rejoice in your saving grace.

6   I will sing to you, O Lord,
    because you have dealt bountifully with me.

Psalm 14[*]

A cry of despair because no-one does good, all claiming there is no God.

1   There is no-one who does good –
    all are corrupt and act abominably.
    They are fools who believe and declare
    that there is no God.

2   While all along the Lord is there,
    observing from heaven
    to see if any among humankind are wise

---

[*] Psalm 14 is the same as Psalm 53, except for a few words, and in place of Yahweh (Lord) El (God) is used. I have put it into different words.

	and searching for him.
3	All of them have lost their way— become totally corrupt. There is no-one who does good, no, not one!
4	They know nothing, all these evildoers, who eat people as they eat bread, and do not acknowledge the Lord.
5	The Lord is with the righteous, and will throw terror among these others.
6	These who would upset the plans of the poor, do they not realize they have the Lord as their refuge?
7	O that deliverance would come from Zion— that the Lord would restore the fortune of his people. Then Jacob's tribe would be glad, Israel's people would rejoice.

Psalm 15

A teaching psalm—only the righteous can live with God

1	Lord, who may live with you? Stay on your holy mountain?
2	Those whose conduct is blameless, who do what is right, who speak truth and mean it.
3	Those who do not use their tongues maliciously, do not bring hurt to their friends, and do not pick a fight with their neighbors.
4	They decry the way of the wicked, and honor those who walk in God's way. They stand by their word, even to their own hurt.

5   Those who do not lend in order to gain,
    and who do not offer nor accept bribes.
    These shall never be shaken.

Psalm 16

God is the God of gods and brings blessings.
(one of the most ancient psalms)

1   Protect me, O Lord,
    for I take refuge in you.

2   I said to the Lord, "You are my God.
    All that is good is in you."

3   I take delight in the holy ones of our land—
    they are the noble ones.

4   I will not name the name of any other god,
    or pour out blood-offerings to them,
    for to choose them would only bring sorrow.

5   The Lord is there for me and will see that I win the day.
    God secures my future.

6   I am delighted with the boundless land that is mine,
    and the wonderful heritage I have.

7   I bless the Lord, who counsels me.
    And even during the night,
    gives me instructions.

8   God, you always go before me,
    and because you lead the way,
    nothing will shake me.

9   This is why I rest secure,
    with glad heart and rejoicing spirit.

10 You do not give me up to death,
    or allow me to enter Sheol.

11   You, O God, show me the path to life.
     In your presence I find joy to the full,
     and, at your right-hand, pleasures
     both now and forever.

Psalm 17

My cause is just, vindicate me and guard me as the apple of your eye

1   My cause is just, O Lord—hear my cry.
     My lips are free from deceit—give ear to my prayer.

2   Vindicate me, O Lord,
     and do what is right for me.

3   Try me—even deep into my heart,
     test me—even far into the night,
     and you will find no evil,
     in word or in deed.

4   I have not done what others do,
     but kept to the words from your lips
     and avoided the way of the violent.

5   My feet have followed your path,
     my steps never swerving.

6   I call upon you, for you will answer me, O God.
     Bend your ear to me and hear my words.

7   Show your steadfast love in wonders,
     for you save from their enemies,
     all who seek refuge at your right hand.

8, 9 Guard me as the apple of your eye,
     from the wicked who would ruin me.
     Hide me in the shadow of your wings,
     from deadly enemies who are all around me.

PSALM 18

| 10 | My enemies' hearts have no pity, |
| | their mouths show their arrogance. |

11, 12 They kept a watch on me and tracked me down.
Now they surround me
like a lion ready to tear me apart,
like a great lion crouching in ambush.

13 Pounce on them, Lord, and overthrow them—
deliver my life from these evil people at war with you.

14 By your hand remove such as these,
who are but mortals,
right out of this world.
As for those whom you cherish,
may they have food in plenty, with enough over
so that even their children and grandchildren are satisfied.

15 Lord, I know that because I do what is right,
I will see you face to face.
Now, when I wake each day,
I am satisfied with catching a glimpse of your likeness.

Psalm 18[*]

A prayer of thanksgiving—God is seen in storm and in victory
over enemies, though depicted as vindictive in triumph.

1 I love you deeply, Lord, you are my strength.

2 Lord, you are my God, my rock,
my fortress and my deliverer.
I trust in you,
I take refuge in you.
You shield me, strengthen me, and save me.

---

[*] Psalm 18 is also found in 2 Sam 22, which is probably why it was traditionally attributed to David on the day when the Lord saved him from the grip of all his enemies and from Saul.

3	You well deserve all my praise, because when I called to you, you rescued me from my enemies.
4	The cords of Sheol wound around me, the torrents of destruction were washing me away,
5	The ropes of hell entangled me, the snares of death were set before me.
6	In my distress I called on the Lord for help. To my God I cried out loud. From his holy palace he heard me— my voice reached his ears.
7	Then the earth started shaking, even the very foundations of the mountains trembled and quaked because God was angry.
8	His nostrils smoked, and his mouth breathed fire as flames from glowing coals flared out.
9	God opened up heaven and came out on dark foaming clouds.
10	God mounted the great winged beast, who carried him down in a flash upon outstretched wings—
11	His cloak the black clouds swollen with water, covering him in the darkness.
12, 13	At God's coming, light flashed before him, hailstones and bolts of fire broke through the clouds, and the voice of the Lord thundered from the heavens.
14	God aimed and shot at the foe and scattered them. He shot great flashes of lightning and routed them.
15	The channels of the sea and the foundations of the earth were exposed to view as he rebuked them.
16, 17	God reached out from on high and drew me out of the waters, delivering me from my enemies,

Psalm 18

      and all who hated me,
      for I was helpless against them.

18   They confronted me,
      but the Lord supported me in calamitous times,

19   The Lord set me down in a wide-open place,
      because he was delighted with me.

20   The Lord rewarded me
      according to the good in me—
      according to how, in his eyes,
      I kept my hands clean.

21   For I have kept the ways of the Lord,
      and not turned aside for any wrongdoing.

22   I kept in mind all the Lord's rules,
      and never put his demands aside.

23   I have kept myself blameless,
      and been free of guilt.

24   Therefore the Lord rewarded me
      according to the good in me -
      according to how, in his eyes,
      I have kept my hands clean.

25   O Lord, you are, with the faithful, faithful,
      and with the blameless, blameless.

26   You are pure with the pure,
      but with the crooked you are crafty.

27   You are there for the humble,
      but bring down the arrogant.

28   You light my lamp, O Lord,
      to give me light in my darkest days.

29   With you I can break through any barricade,
      and leap right over a wall.

30   This is my God,
      the one true to his promises
      and perfect in all his ways.

Psalm 18

31 Who really is this God—
this God who is a rock on which we can stand?

32 Who gives us strength?
Who secures our paths?
Who is this God
except Yahweh, the Lord?

33 He made my feet like a deer's feet,
secure even on the heights.

34, 35 He has given me the training I need,
and the strength of hands and arms
to fight the enemy,
and been my shield to save me when I needed it.
God stooped down to help,
and in so doing made me great.

36 He gave me long-striding legs and strong ankles,
so that I did not slip and fall.

37* I chased after my enemies and caught up with them.
I attacked them, destroying them all.

38 I pounded them till I was sure they would not get up again.
They lay totally flattened under my feet.

39 It was you, Lord, who gave me the strength to do this,
you who made them submissive to me.

40 You showed me where my enemy was most vulnerable,
so that I could finish them off.

41 They cried out for help, but there was no-one to rescue them.
They even cried to you, but you gave no answer.

42 Then I pummeled them to dust,
and they were blown away as chaff before the wind,

43 You made me triumph over the revolt of the people,
and made me ruler over the nonbelievers.
My servants are now those
whom I never came across before.

* The section, from verses 37 to 50, is one I was sorely tempted to leave out of the book. It is so full of vindictive violence against the enemy, that it appalled me. Yet it is in the Scriptures and surely has its place.

44	Now when people hear of me, they immediately obey me, and foreigners cringe before me.
45	Foreigners surrender without a fight because they are afraid.
46	The Lord lives, praise to my rock. I exalt the God who rescued me.
47	It is you, O God, who avenged me, and subjected all these people to me.
48	You are the one who set me free from all my enemies. You are the one who has now set me above all those violent men.
49	This is why I give thanks to you, O God, among all those who do not believe. This is why I praise your name.
50	O God, you have brought great victory to your king. You have shown unmerited mercy to your anointed, to David and his descendants for ever.

Psalm 19

In praise of creation, and in praise of God's law

1	The immensity of space surrounding us, and the sky arching over us proclaim the glory of the Creator.
2	Day after day they speak to us, night after night they inform us,
3	Without using words, without making a speech.
4a	Yet throughout the world they are heard. Around the globe they are listened to.

PSALM 19

4b–6	The sky stretching above us is like a wedding canopy for the sun who comes out like a bridegroom rejoicing. It is like a tent for the sun, who emerges from it every morning, and like an athlete running his course, goes from one end of the earth to the other— pouring its heat on everything in its path.
7	Just so the Law of the Lord is perfect, bringing new life to my soul. The decrees of the Lord are sure, bringing wisdom to my mind,
8	The precepts of the Lord are right, giving joy to my heart. The commands of the Lord are straight-forward, bringing light to my eyes.
9	The edicts of God are pure, enduring forever. The judgements of God are truth, every one of them just.
10	They are more desirable than gold, even large quantities of the most refined gold, They are sweeter than honey dripping from the honeycomb.
11	They enlighten your servant— keeping them brings great reward.
12	Who is aware of all their own faults? Forgive me for the sins I do not see.
13	Keep me from sinning willfully— may these sins never gain the upper hand. Then I shall be blameless and clear of any great failing.

14   May the words that I utter
be what you desire,
and the thoughts deep within my heart
be what you want from me,
O Lord, my rock and my redeemer.

Psalm 20

A Blessing

1   May the Lord be with you when you are in trouble.
May the God of Jacob and Rachel protect you.

2   May God send you help from his sanctuary,
and strength for you out of his holy city.

3   May God remember the sacrifices you have made,
and take delight in the gifts that you have offered him.

4   May God grant you your heart's desire,
and make all your plans come to pass.

5   May God make all your dreams come true.
Then we will all rejoice and celebrate your victory.

6   For I know that God will help those whom he has called.
He will answer their requests,
and help them triumph over their enemies.

7   Others may look to worldly alliances,
and the build-up of arms for strength.

8   They will all fail.
But we will overcome.
For we rely on the Lord our God,
and we will be standing strong to the end,

9   Save us, Lord!
Hear us when we call to you.

Psalm 21

*Praise-song to the king, who with God's backing,
wipes out his enemies.*

1	O Lord, the king will delight in your strength, and find great joy in your saving power.
2	You have given him what he desired, and did not refuse what he asked of you.
3	You gave him the gift of prosperity— you placed a crown of pure gold on his head.
4	He asked you to give him life, and you gave it to him— length of days stretching out forever.
5	Great is his glory through your victory. You gave him honor and majesty besides.
6	The blessings you gave will last forever, and your presence will cheer him immensely.
7	The king trusts in the Lord, and so, in God's mercy, he will stand firm.
8	God will lend a hand in identifying all his enemies, making known those who hate him.
9	The Lord will swallow them up in anger, make them burn in a fiery kiln, and be consumed in the fire.
10	Whatever they produce will cease to exist, even their progeny will be annihilated.
11	For they plotted evil against you, hatched a malicious plan, although they were unable to carry it out.
12	You will fire straight at them, making them turn and flee.
13	May your own strength exalt you, O Lord, as we sing praises to your power.

Psalm 22.

*A lament, starting with feeling forsaken by God,
which was quoted by Jesus on the cross.*

1   O God, my God, why have you forsaken me?
         Why have you distanced yourself from me—
         and from my groans?

2   O God, I cry out by day and get no answer,
         by night and get no response.

3, 4   You are a holy God.
         Our ancestors trusted you, and you delivered them.
         They enthroned you in praise.

5   They cried to you, and you saved them.
         They trusted you and you did not let them down.

6, 7   But look at me! I am like a worm,
         hardly human anymore.
         I am despised by others, mocked to my face,
         called names and scorned.

8   My faith in you is flung back at me,
         "So you have faith in God?
         Let him save you if he loves you so much!"

9, 10   O God, I have been yours from the beginning.
         You helped give me birth.
         You protected me while I was still at my mother's breast.
         I have been dedicated to you ever since.

11   So do not abandon me now.
         Trouble is near,
         and no-one can help but you.

12, 13   My enemy surrounds me like a herd of bulls,
         circling like the bulls of Bashan,
         their jaws like those of a lion ready to strike.

14   I am on fire,
         my sweat like water being poured out,
         my heart melting like wax,
         while my bones are falling apart joint by joint.

PSALM 22.

15–17	My throat is as dry as an empty pot in the sun— my tongue sticks to the roof of my mouth. Even my hands and feet are shrunk and wrinkled, and my bones are so visible I can count them. Is this the dust of death?
16a	Evildoers surround me like a pack of dogs circling. They have bound me, hand and foot.
18	They are already at my clothing— casting lots for the choice garments, dividing the rest among themselves.
19	So Lord, my strength, come quickly to my aid— do not keep your distance.
20	Deliver me from the sword. Save me from lions and dogs,
21a	and from the horns of the bull.
21b	God, you did indeed come to my aid. You snatched me from the horns of the bull.
24	You did not turn your back on me, nor say that I deserved my affliction, but you listened to my pleas.
23	All those who worship the Lord, praise him! Give him the glory, children of Jacob and Rachel! Come in awe before him, children of Israel!
22,25	In the midst of all the people assembled, I give God praise! I pay my vows before those who worship God.
26	Those who seek God shall find him and praise him. Even the poor will come and eat and be satisfied, their hearts alive forever.
27	Indeed, the whole earth from end to end will remember our Lord and turn to him. From every nation they will come and worship him.

28	They all belong to the Lord,
	who rules over every one of them.
29	Even those whose sleep is under the earth,
	will come to worship the Lord,
	those whose covering is the dust of the earth,
	will kneel before him.
	For the Victor himself restores to life.
30	And those yet to be born will serve him.
	Generations stretching endlessly into the future
	will be told about God,
31	And, yet unborn, will proclaim his saving power,
	saying that God does everything that is done.

Psalm 23

The Good Shepherd

1	Lord, with you as my shepherd,
	what more could I want?
2	You lead me along the right path,
	resting in green pastures,
	drinking from fresh, still waters.
3	You restore me, body and soul,
	for that is your nature.
4	Even as I walk through a valley dark as death,
	I am not afraid—of this or any other threat,
	for you, O God, are with me,
	your shepherd's staff ready to guide and comfort me.
5	You prepare a feast for me
	and place me in the seat of honor,
	in the very presence of my enemies.
	My cup of blessings is brimming over.

6   Surely goodness and mercy will be with me all my days,
as now and forever I live in the presence of my Lord.

Psalm 24

Song of Praise to the Creator and a Processional Song

1, 2   The earth belongs to God—
the whole universe,
to God who made it—
the seas, the land with its rivers,
and every living creature in it.

3   Who can approach the mountain of the Lord?
Who can come into God's holy place?

4   Those whose hearts are pure,
whose hands are clean—
those who have no duplicity,
nothing false about them.

5   The Lord will bless them,
our savior God will vindicate them.

6   And it is this generation who look for God,
who yearn to meet God face to face.

(Processional Song)

7   Part 1: Lift up your heads, you temple gates!
Open up, you everlasting doors,
The King of Glory is coming in.

8   Part 2: Who is this King of glory?

Part 1; The Lord, strong and mighty,
The Lord, mighty in battle.

9   Part 1: Lift up your heads, you temple gates!
Open up, you everlasting doors!
The King of glory is coming in.

10	Part 2: Who is this King of glory?
	Part 1: The Lord Almighty— He is the King of Glory!

Psalm 25

A prayer asking for forgiveness and protection
(Originally an acrostic psalm)

1	I turn with my whole being towards you, O Lord.
2, 3	I put my trust in you. Do not let shame fall on me, or on others who seek your presence. But may those who intentionally cause harm fail, and be fully shamed.
4, 5	Guide me along your way, O Lord. Teach me the truth, and help me to walk in it. For you are God, my savior, I long for you day in and day out.
6	Be full of compassion and mercy, O Lord, as you are, and always have been.
7	Do not let the folly of my youth spring to mind, or any of my recent failures, but regard me in the light of your everlasting love and goodness.
8	For you, Lord, are all goodness and righteousness, as you call the wayward back to the right path.
9	You lead the humble in your way, showing them what is right.
10	For your way, Lord, to those who stick to it and honor your covenant, is full of compassion and faithfulness.

11	O Lord, for the sake of your name, forgive my sins—and I have sinned badly.
12	What of those who revere you, Lord? You will show them the way they should follow.
13	Then they will know prosperity, and their children will possess the land.
14	God, you will befriend those who hold you in awe— they are the ones who will covenant with you
15	I keep my eyes on you, Lord at all times, for you will pull me out of any net that entangles me.
16-18	O Lord, I feel anguish and loneliness. I am distressed and full of trouble— look and see for yourself. Forgive me all my sins and clear my heart of all that troubles me.
19	Surely you can see all those who are against me— those who hate me with such vitriol.
20	I look to you for refuge. Do not let me be put to shame, but guard me and keep me safe.
21	Preserve me in your integrity and righteousness, for my hope is in you.
21	Redeem Israel out of all its troubles, O God.

Psalm 26

I am true in my whole being

1	Vindicate me, O Lord, for I have walked in integrity, and I have trusted you without wavering.

2	Try me, O Lord, and test me— in body, mind, and spirit. You will find me true throughout.
3	I always hold before me your steadfast love. I walk in your truth.
4	I steer clear of those who flaunt your law, those who say they follow it, but do not.
5	I hate the company of those that do wrong, and will not associate with evildoers.
6,7	For I keep my hands clean, and come to your table in the sanctuary singing songs of thanksgiving, and telling others what you have done for me.
8	I love your house, O Lord— the place where your presence is felt and your glory sensed.
9	See me for what I am – a person of integrity.
10	Do not class me among the ones who are corrupt or blood-thirsty, ignoring you and your ways.
11, 12	I walk in your straight way— save me and be merciful to me. Among the multitude who call on you, I am there, singing your praises, and blessing you.

Psalm 27

On putting trust in God and waiting for him—knowing no fear

1	The Lord is my light and my salvation— Who then shall I fear?

He is the fortress of my life.
Who could make me afraid?

2 My enemies are out to make a meal of me—
Those evildoers!
They are the ones who will stumble and fall.

3 If an army is set to attack,
my heart would not quake in fear.
Even if war breaks out around me,
I will know no fear,
I will confidently hold my ground.

4 I ask one thing of the Lord—
one thing that I long for,
that I may live with the Lord where he lives
my whole life long—
to feast on the beauty of the Lord,
and to drink in his presence where he sits in glory.

5 I can rest assured that when trouble comes,
God will hide me in his dwelling place
and place me out of reach on a high rock.

6 Then with my enemies far below,
safe in his house,
I will give my all to God,
with singing and joyous celebration.

7 Hear, O Lord, when I cry to you.
Be gracious to me and answer.

8 From deep in my heart,
I yearn to find you
and meet you face to face.

9 Do not turn your back on me in anger.
Do not push me aside or abandon me,
O God, my savior.

10 Even if my father or my mother abandon me,
you, Lord, will hold on to me.

11 O Lord, teach me your way,
and lead me along your level path,
in full sight of those against me.

| 12 | Do not let my enemies
get the better of me,
for they have set up false witnesses,
and threaten violence. |
| 13 | I remain confident of this—
I will experience the goodness of the Lord
in the land of the living. |
| 14 | So wait for the Lord.
With a strong and confident hope,
wait for the Lord. |

Psalm 28

A confident plea to God for help

| 1 | O Lord, you are my rock,
but do not be as deaf as a rock when I call to you,
for if you are silent in response,
it will be a death-knoll to me. |
| 2 | Listen to my plea,
as I cry to you for help,
my whole body reaching out to you. |
| 3 | Do not put me in the same category as the wicked,
those whose deeds are evil,
who pretend to be a friend,
while harboring malice in their hearts. |
| 4,5 | Give them their due reward,
evil for evil.
Pay them what they deserve—
what their evil has earned.
Since they care nothing for what you have done,
but only want to destroy it,
destroy them—and permanently. |

6   But praise be to you, Lord!
  You did hear my pleas.
  You did respond to my cries.

7   My heart leaps for joy,
  and my tongue bursts into songs of thanksgiving.
  O Lord, you are my strength and my protection,
  I trust you from the bottom of my heart.
  You have renewed my life.

8   You are the strength of all your people,
  and the savior of those you call.

9   Lord, be a shepherd to your people.
  Save them and keep them safe,
  and bless them forever.

Psalm 29

The storm is the vehicle of God's power
(One of the older of the psalms)

1   Let all the children of God
  praise the Lord for his glory and strength.

2   Let them all worship God
  in the beauty of his holiness,
  giving him the glory he deserves.

3   See God's power in the power of a storm.
  Hear his voice in the crashing of the waves,

4   His voice both powerful and majestic,

5   God's voice powerful enough to bring
  the mighty cedar crashing down,

6   And to whip through the forests
  of Lebanon and Mount Hermon,
  making the trees frolic like young calves.

7,8	The Lord God's voice reverberates through the wilderness, flashing fire and shaking the ground. It spins the oak trees around. It strips them of their leaves.
9	We watch in awe and give God the glory.
10	The Lord is King for all time, from before the great flood, till time itself ends.
11	May the Lord God bless his people with strength, and give them peace.

Psalm 30

*Praise for being healed and spared from death,
and for joy that comes with the morning*

1	I will hold you high in my heart, O Lord, for you lifted me out of the depths and did not let my grief utterly overwhelm me.
2	O Lord, my God, I called to you to help me and you made me whole again.
3	You brought me from the grave. You prevented me from giving in totally to despair.
4	So all who are faithful to our Lord, sing songs of praise, pray prayers of thanks.
5	God's anger lasts but for a moment, God's bounty a whole life long. You may weep through the night, but joy will come with the morning.
6	O Lord, when I was in your care my world stood firm,

| | I felt secure and said, |
| | "I will never be shaken." |

7   But then you turned your back on me,
and I was filled with dismay.

8-10   I cried to you, Lord, pleading my cause,
"How will my death profit you?
If I am dead and buried, will the dust praise you?
Will it tell how faithful you are?
Listen to my plea—
be gracious to me—
turn to me and help me."

11,12   O Lord my God,
you have turned my weeping into dancing—
you swopped my burial clothes for clothes of celebration.
My heart sings within me—
refuses to be silent.
I will never stop thanking you.

Psalm 31

A prayer for help, ending with thanks to God for helping the just and punishing the wicked

1,2   O Lord, free me, rescue me, listen to my plea,
for I have taken refuge in you.
In your faithfulness do not let me be put to shame—
be my rock of safety, my fortress of strength.

3   You are indeed my rock and my fortress—
lead me and guide me.

4   Free me from the trap that is set for me,
for you are my rescuer.

5   Into your hands I commit my spirit.
O faithful God, O God of truth,
save me.

Psalm 31

6   I spurn those who put their trust in vaporous lies.
      My trust is in you, O Lord.

7   O my God, I rejoice and celebrate your constant love,
      for you have seen what troubled me,
      and the anguish of my soul.

8   You did not hand me over to evil people,
      but you set my feet on firm ground
      with plenty of room to maneuver.

9   Be gracious to me O Lord,
      I am in distress.
      My eyes are worn down with tears,
      along with my very self.

10   Sorrow is my way of life,
      sighing my companion,
      misery siphons off my strength,
      and my bones waste away.

11   My adversaries scorn me,
      my neighbors avoid me,
      my friends dread being with me,
      and strangers cross to the other side of the street.

12   Like one long dead
      they have forgotten me,
      they have discarded me like a broken vessel.

13   Yet I still hear to my horror
      how they whisper together,
      plotting to end my life.

14   But I trust, O Lord, in you,
      for you are my God—
      each stage of my life is in your hands.

15–17 Deliver me out of the enemy's clutches.
      Look with favor on your servant.
      Save me in your steadfast love.
      Do not let me suffer shame, I beg you.
      May it be the wicked who are put to shame,
      who end up dumbfounded in Sheol.

18 May lips that tell lies,
    lips that speak dismissively against the just,
    with a haughty, contemptuous attitude,
    be silenced.

19 But for those who revere you,
    who take refuge in you,
    how different their fate—
    you shower them with goodness.

20 Your presence is a shelter
    where you hide them from the intrigues of others,
    your house a place of safety
    from the war of words.

21 Blessed be our Lord,
    for he showered his wonderful love on me
    when I felt as though I was hemmed in on all sides.

22 When I was under threat,
    when I thought I had been driven out of God's sight,
    like a city under siege, I cried out for help,
    and God heard my pleas.

23 Love the Lord,
    all you, his faithful ones.
    The Lord preserves the faithful
    and gives the arrogant what they deserve,

24 So be strong and take heart,
    all you who hope in the Lord.

Psalm 32

Confession of sin brings forgiveness and joy

1 How happy are those who have been forgiven
   for the wrongs they have done—
   whose sin has been wiped away.

Psalm 32

2   How happy are those the Lord declares
    innocent in all their actions,
    whose spirit has no duplicity.

3   When I kept quiet about my guilt,
    my body wasted away,
    and I felt miserable all day long.

4   For day and night, I felt your hand heavy on me, O Lord,
    drying up my strength,
    as the heat of summer drains my energy.

5   Then I confessed my sin to you—I hid nothing from you,
    since I determined I must be honest before you.
    You forgave me the guilt of my sin.

6   All who have faith in God,
    can come before him and pray in time of need,—
    so the rushing waters will not overwhelm him.*

7   You are my hiding place when I am in trouble.
    I will soon be crying out, not in distress,
    but in joy at being rescued.

8   God promises,
    "I will teach you the way you should live,
    I will look out for you and counsel you.

9   So do not be like a horse or donkey who understands nothing,
    who needs a bit and bridle
    to keep him on track and of use to you."

10 The wicked encounter many torments,
    but constant love surrounds
    those who are faithful to the Lord,

11 So you who are faithful and just, be of good cheer,
    you whose hearts are pure, sing for joy!

---

* It is thought that vs 6 has been inserted into this psalm at a later date. It does not fit as it is, being written as prose.

Psalm 33

A hymn of praise to the Creator and the God who is involved with us

1. Rejoice in the Lord—all good and upright people!
   Praise him for he is praiseworthy indeed.
2. Praise the Lord with music—
   praise him on stringed instruments.
3. Sing a new song to God, your voices raised
   with the whole orchestra, in joyous harmony.
4. The word of the Lord is straight and true.
   He is faithful in everything he does.
5. His constant love fills the whole world—
   his love shown to us in what is right and just.
6. The Lord made the sky above us, by uttering his word—
   all the stars by breathing on them.
7. The seas he made as we would gather water in a bowl,
   and fresh water he put in deep storehouses.
8. Let all creatures fear the Lord,
   all people stand in awe of him,
9. For he spoke into being all that is,
   he commanded and it stayed in place.
10. He can frustrate the scheming of the nations –
    bring to nothing what people are planning.
11. But the plans of God remain constant forever,
    the designs of his mind last through all generations.

12. The nation who has the Lord as their God are a happy people—
    the ones whom God has chosen as his own.
13. The Lord looks out from heaven.
    He sees the whole of humankind.
14. From his dwelling place God watches
    all the earth's inhabitants.

Psalm 34

15   He made each one,
    and can see into their hearts and observe their deeds.

16   A nation does not conquer by the might of its army,
    and a soldier is not saved by his own strength.

17   The machinery of war does not win the battle,
    no matter how powerful—it cannot save.

18   For truly, God keeps his eye on those who worship him,
    those who trust in his constant love,

19   So that he can keep them alive through times of famine,
    and deliver them from death.

20   O Lord, we wait for you,
    for you are our help and protection.

21   You give us joy
    because we trust in you,

22   Keep us constantly in your love,
    for we put our hope in you.

Psalm 34

A teaching psalm with thanksgiving for God's help for the righteous and destruction of the wicked. Originally an acrostic poem

1   I will extol the Lord at all times—
   I will continually voice God's praise.

2   My soul makes its boast in the Lord.
   When the humble hear of this they rejoice.

3   Come, join me in lifting up the Lord—
   in exalting our God together.

4   I searched for the Lord—
   who listened to me and took away all my fears.

PSALM 34

5 Look to God and your faces will radiate
   joy and not shame.

6 Poor you may be, but when you cry to God,
   he will save you from all your troubles,

7 and will send angels to the rescue
   of everyone who worships God.

8 Taste and drink deeply—see that the Lord is sweet,
   and brings joy to those who trust in him.

9 Hold God in awe, all of you, his holy ones,
   then you shall want for nothing.

10 The rich will come to suffer hunger and thirst,
   but those who look to God have all they need.

11 Gather around me, children,
   and I will teach you the way of the Lord.

12 Which of you longs for life?
   For long days in which to enjoy it?

13 Then keep your tongue from hurtful speech,
   and your lips from uttering deceit.

14 Turn your back on evil and do good.
   Look for peace and go after it.

15 The Lord keeps an eye on the upright.
   and both ears attentive to their cry.

16 The Lord turns his back on evildoers,
   and even expunges all memory of them from the earth.

17 If those who do what is right cry to the Lord,
   they will be heard and plucked
   out of what troubles them.

18 The Lord is close to the broken-hearted
   and saves those whose spirit is crushed.

19 The just may go through many trials,
   but the Lord will rescue them from them all,

20	And will take care of them, right through to their bones—
	not one will be broken.
21	Evil will itself turn on the wicked and kill them.
	Those who despise the just
	will themselves be condemned.
22	The Lord redeems the soul of those who serve,
	and allows none of those who trust in him
	to be condemned.

Psalm 35

A plea for exoneration on a trumped-up charge

1	O Lord, take up the fight against those who fight with me.
	Take on those who have issue with me.
2, 3	Take up your weapons and come to my aid.
	Stop my pursuers in their tracks,
	and assure me that you are my savior.
4	May those who seek my life
	be confounded and put to shame—
	those who want to harm me
	retreat in confusion.
5	Let them be as chaff blown away by the wind,
	with the angel of the Lord driving them.
6	May their way be dark and slippery,
	with the angel of the Lord still hot on their heels.
7	They set their nets for me without a reason,
	they dug a deep pit for me without a cause.
8	Let them be the ones ensnared in their own nets,
	the ones who fall into their own pit,
	so that ruin comes suddenly upon them.

Psalm 35

9   Then I will exult in you, Lord,
    and rejoice in your deliverance.

10 My whole being will cry out,
    "O Lord, is there anyone like you?
    You deliver the weak
    from their stronger oppressors,
    the frail and needy
    from those who steal what little they have."

11 They brought false witnesses against me
    in a charge of which I knew nothing.

12 They repaid me evil for good,
    so that my soul was bereft.

13 Yet when this same enemy became sick,
    I put on mourning clothes,
    I fasted till I suffered,
    I prayed till I was exhausted,

14 It was as though my own friend or brother were ill,
    even as though it were my own mother.

15, 16 But when I stumbled,
    they came together and laughed at me.
    Like strangers I had never seen before
    they tore into me,
    grinning at me and mocking me to my face.

17 How long must this go on, Lord?
    Come and rescue me from this pack of liars.

18 Then I will give you thanks in the assembly of your people—
    praise you before a huge crowd.

19 O Lord, do not let my lying enemies
    rejoice at my expense,
    or those who hate me for no reason
    have the upper hand.

20 They speak peace, but mean the opposite,
    speak words meant to deceive the peace-loving person.

21	They spread rumors about me. Blatant lies! Claiming, "Yes indeed! We saw it with our own eyes."
22	You can clearly see all this, O Lord. Do not remain silent, Do not keep your distance,
23	But wake up! Come forward with the right defense.
24	As my God and my Lord, judge me yourself, and vindicate me according to your righteousness. Do not let them rejoice over me.
25	Do not let them say, "We got what we wanted." or claim, "We have swallowed him up."
26	May those who wanted to rejoice at my downfall, be themselves confounded and brought low.
27	And may those who desired to see me vindicated, celebrate in joy and gladness, shouting, "Great are you, Lord! because you delight in the well-being of your servants."
28	My voice will be raised with theirs in telling of your righteousness, and praising you all day long.

Psalm 36

In praise of God's loving-kindness, and how evil and good respond

1	Evil begins deep in the heart of the wicked, because they have no fear of God.
2	They are arrogant enough to believe that their wicked deeds will not be found out and hated.

3   Their words are deceitful and hurtful—
their deeds show no goodness or wisdom.

4   They are set in their way of wrongdoing,
even plotting evil while in bed,
instead of rejecting it.

5   But your constant love, O Lord,
is great enough to extend throughout the universe.
Your faithfulness encompasses us like clouds,

6   Your righteousness is higher than the highest mountain,
your justice deeper than the deepest sea,
and you include both humans and animals
in your salvation.

7   O God, your constant love is so precious,
it extends to everybody—
each and every person can find shelter under your wings.

8   They take their fill from the abundance in your house,
they drink from the river of your delights.

9   In you is the very fountain of life.
In your light we see light.

10   O continue to love constantly those who love you,
and to save those with an upright heart.

11   Do not let the arrogant kick me around,
or the wicked push me aside.

12   Bur rather may the wicked lie prostrate.
May evildoers be thrown down,
unable to rise again.

Psalm 37*

*A teaching psalm which shows how those who do good prosper,
but those who do wrong will in the end lose everything*

* Psalm 37 is an acrostic psalm with two lines to every letter of the alphabet.

Psalm 37

1. Do not fret because evildoers get away with it,
   or be envious of them,
2. For they will soon fade like the grass,
   and wither like a green herb at noon.
3. Trust in the Lord and do good,
   then you will have land to live in and food to eat.
4. Delight in the Lord,
   and he will give you your heart's desire.
5. Commit your way to the Lord,
   put your trust in him, and he will act,
6. Making your good name shine like the morning light,
   and the justice of your cause like the sun at noon.
7. Be still before the Lord and wait patiently for him.
   Do not be upset when the dishonest prosper
   while carrying out their evil schemes.
8. Do not be angry, do not rage over them,
   do not even get irritated—it can only lead to evil.
9. The wicked will be cut off,
   but those who wait patiently for the Lord—
   they will inherit the land.
10. Wait for a while and the wicked shall be no more.
    You may search for their place—it has vanished.
11. But the meek shall inherit the land and be full of joy
    at the abundance of peace they have.
12. The wicked plot against the good,
    they sneer at them,
13. But the Lord can see that their day of reckoning is coming,
    so he laughs at them in derision.
14. The wicked have their weapons aimed at the poor and the needy
    and at those who walk uprightly.
15. Their swords will pierce their own hearts—
    their weapons will malfunction.

16 Better is the little that the right-living person has,
than the wealth the evildoer has amassed.

17 For the Lord will break the hold they have on riches—
it is the righteous person who will prosper.

18 The Lord knows how the upright live each day,
their heritage will last forever.

19 When evil times come, they will not be ashamed.
In days of great want, they will have more than they need.

20 But the wicked will have vanished.
The enemies of the Lord will be like the grass in spring—
soon gone.
They will be like smoke blown away.

21 The wicked borrow and do not pay back,
while the righteous are generous and keep on giving.

22 Those blessed by the Lord shall inherit the land,
and those cursed by him shall be cut off.

23 When we follow the Lord's way,
he makes our steps sure.

24 He holds our hand, which prevents us,
though we stumble, from falling headlong.

25 Once I was young and now I am old.
In all that time I have never seen
the right-living person forsaken,
or their offspring begging.

26 On the contrary, they are the ones
able to give liberally and lend.
Their children too, become a blessing.

27 Turn from evil and do what is right,
then you will always live securely.

28 For the Lord loves justice.
He will not abandon those faithful to him.

29 Those living good, right and just lives,
shall inherit the land and live in it forever.

30	The upright with their mouths speak wisdom, with their tongues, justice,
31	While in their hearts is the law of the Lord, so that their feet will not slip.
32	The wicked watch good people and plot to bring them down.
33	The Lord will not abandon them to their power, or let them be condemned.
34	Wait for the Lord. Keep following his way. He will lift you up and ultimately you will inherit the whole earth. You will see the wicked end up with nothing.
35	At one time I can see the wicked in power, spreading like a fast-growing tree,
36	At another time they are no more— no matter how hard I look, they are nowhere to be found.
37	Take note of the upright, and look closely at the honest. They will find peace.
38	All those that flout the law will be destroyed— their inheritance will be cut off.
39	Salvation will come to the upright through the Lord, for he is their refuge whenever they are in trouble.
40	And because they trust in him, the Lord will help them and save them. He will free them from the wicked.

Psalm 38

*A desperate plea for forgiveness because
"there is not one spot in me that is sound"*

1	O Lord, do not rebuke me in anger, or punish me in wrath,
2	For your arrows have pierced me and your hand is pressing me down.
3	There is no health in my flesh because you are angry, no soundness in my bones because of my own wrongdoing.
4	I am way over my head in my sins— they are a burden too heavy to bear.
5	My wounds continue to fester and spread their infection throughout my body, all because of my foolishness.
6	I suffer deep depression. I am filled all day with a numbing sorrow.
7	There is not one spot in me that is sound.
8	Because this anguish is deep within my heart, I am utterly crushed.
9	Lord, you know what I am going through— none of my distress escapes your gaze.
10	My heart is aching, and my strength has vanished. Even the light has gone from my eyes.
11, 12	Everyone keeps their distance, friends, acquaintances, and neighbors, except those who want my life— they confer with each other on how to ruin me completely.
13, 14	I am mostly oblivious to this— I am like a deaf person who hears nothing, a mute person who makes no retort.

PSALM 39

15	I put all my hope in you, my Lord, my God, I wait for you to answer me.
16, 17	I long for you to listen to me, I ask you not to let my foes rejoice over me, when my foot slips again,
18	For it is so easy to stumble, to do something wrong, even though I intend good.
19	My enemies have multiplied in number and strength. They hate me without cause.
20	My adversaries are those who return evil for good. They slander me when I try to do the right thing.
21	Do not abandon me, O Lord, do not distance yourself from me. O my Lord, God of my salvation, come quickly to my aid.

PSALM 39

An attempt to keep quiet because life seems to have no meaning

1	I was determined to keep my tongue from causing me to sin, so I decided, when I saw what crooked people got away with, I would zip my mouth.
2	I did keep quiet, but not saying a word did not help— my distress only grew.
3	I became more and more heated— a fire burning within me. So I spoke out.

Psalm 39

4   Lord, let me know how long my life will be,
       so that I can see how insignificant it is.

5   It is a mere handsbreadth,
       a mere nothing in your sight,
       even at best, it is meaningless.

6   Surely everyone's life is but a shadow—
       we all worry about nothing.
       Even those who heap up riches die,
       and someone else reaps the benefit.

7   Now Lord, what is there to hope for?
       All I can hope for is in you.

8   Do not allow me to become the scorn of the fool.
       Take away my leaning towards evil.

9   All that has happened to me is your doing.
       I am speechless before it.
       I have not a word to say.

10   Your hand has flattened me completely—
       I beg you to stop striking me.

11   You strike down humans in retaliation for sin,
       taking from them what they value most—
       as though every person's life were meaningless.

12   Hear my cry, O Lord,
       respond to my tears,
       listen to my prayer.
       I am just a foreigner passing through,
       a stranger seeking hospitality,
       as my ancestors did.

13   Show mercy to me,
       Let me recover my sense of purpose
       before I leave this life and am no more.

Psalm 40

Rescued from enemies after waiting patiently for the Lord

1	I waited patiently for the Lord.
	The Lord turned and looked at me,
	and listened to my cry.
2	God lifted me out of the pit of desolation—
	pulled me out of the clinging mud,
	set my feet on a rock,
	and gave me a secure place to stand.
3	The Lord gave me a new song to sing—
	a praise-song to my God.
	Many will see with wonder what you have done, O God,
	and put their trust in you.
4	Happy are those who trust in you,
	and not in idols, nor in others who make false promises.
5	O God, there are so many wonderful things you have done,
	multiplying over and over your goodness to us,
	so many, that when I try to count them,
	I cannot get anywhere close.
6	What can I do in return?
	You do not want sacrifices made or deeds performed.
	I know because you gave me a way
	to listen for your instructions.
7, 8	It is written in the great book,
	which includes me as well as others,
	that God wants us rather to take his words to heart,
	and to find joy in doing what he desires.
9, 10	In the great assembly of all your people,
	I gladly spoke of your way of deliverance.
	You know, Lord, that I have not held back—
	not kept your righteousness for myself,
	Not hidden your faithfulness and salvation,
	nor concealed your constant love from anyone else.

11 Do not Lord, withhold your mercy from me.
    May your loving kindness,
    and your truth continually keep me safe.

12 I am in trouble,
    for my sins, too many to number,
    more even than the hairs on my head,
    have caught up with me,
    so that I cannot see straight.
    My heart is failing.

13* Please, Lord, lift them from me.
     Come quickly and set me free.

14 And may those trying to snatch my life from me
    be ashamed of themselves and full of confusion.
    Those who wish me evil, be halted in their tracks,
    and be themselves overwhelmed with shame.

15 May those who clap their hands saying,
    "Yay! Yay!" at my shame,
    be appalled because of their own humiliation.

16 On the other hand, may all those who seek you
    find joy and gladness in you.
    May they all together say, "God is great!"

17 Poor and needy as I am,
    I know that you think of me.
    You are my helper and my rescuer.
    Do not wait any longer with that help,
    O my God.

Psalm 41

A prayer for healing and for victory over the enemy, who was once a friend

1 Happy are those who care for the poor.
   The Lord will rescue them
   when they are in trouble.

---

* The words of Ps 40:13 – 17, with a few differences, are the same as Ps 70. I have rendered them differently

Psalm 41

2	They are the blessed of the earth, for the Lord keeps them alive and safe. The Lord will not leave them at the mercy of their enemies.
3	If they do fall ill, God will heal them, and return them to full health.
4	I had sinned against God and suffered in consequence. I prayed, "O God, in your mercy, heal my soul."
5	My enemy thought I was being punished for my sins, that I would soon die, and my name be forgotten.
6–8	One of them pretended to be friendly when he visited me, but he was just gathering information, which he used to speak ill of me to others. Those who hate me whisper together, planning to hurt me. They are sure I will not rise from my sickbed.
9	Even my trusted friend, so dear to me, with whom I shared my bread, has walked out on me.
10	But, please Lord, be gracious to me and heal me, so that I can turn the tables on them.
11	I know that you are still pleased with me, because my enemy has not yet triumphed over me.
12	You have seen my integrity and kept me going, placing me in your very presence forever.
13	Blessed be the Lord God of Israel, who is from before time was, till after time ceases to be.
	[Amen and Amen]—These words end Book I of the psalter.

BOOK II

Psalms 42–72

in which Elohim (God) is used and not Yahweh (Lord)

Psalm 42[*]

Trusting in God while feeling depressed

1. As the deer longs for a flowing stream,
   so my soul longs for you, O God,

2. My whole being thirsts for God,
   for you, the living God.
   When will I again be aware of your presence?

3. I have been living on tears for food,
   while others say to me,
   "Where is this God of yours?"

4. Into my mind springs the memory
   of going with the masses on holy days,
   of leading the procession to the house of God—
   all of us shouting in thanks and praise.

5. *O my soul, why so depressed?*
   Why cast down to the depths?
   Put your hope in God, your savior,
   for you will live to praise God yet again.

6. Dear God, my soul has hit the depths within me.
   I can only rely on my memory of you

---

[*] It is thought that originally Psalm 42 and Psalm 43 formed one psalm

        from the land of Jordan,
        and from the heights of Hermon and the hill Mizar.

7   Deep calls to deep at the roaring of your waterfalls.
        All your surging waters, wave after wave,
        have gone over me.

8   Still by day your constant love is in command,
        and at night I sing your song,
        a prayer to the God of my life.

9   Yet I say to God, my rock,
        why have you forgotten me?
        Why leave me in sorrow because of
        the way my enemies oppress me?

10   They taunt me, saying,
        "Where is this God of yours?"
        It is like a festering wound to my body.

11   *O my soul, why so depressed?*
        Why cast down to the depths?
        Put your hope in God, your savior,
        for you will live to praise God yet again.*

Psalm 43

Continuing the theme of Psalm 42

1   Plead my case, O God, and pronounce me innocent.
        Set me free from those who are deceitful and crooked.

2   You are the God who strengthens me.
        Why am I in such agony
        from the way my enemies oppress me?

---

* It is thought that originally Psalm 42 and Psalm 43 formed one psalm

3   Send out your light and your truth—
    let them be my guide.
    Let them bring me to the holy place
    where you live.

4   I will go to your altar, O God,
    my joy and my delight,
    where I will praise you joyfully,
    with harp and song, O God, my God.

5   *O my soul, why so depressed?*
    Why cast down to the depths?
    Put your hope in God, your savior,
    for you will live to praise him yet again.

Psalm 44

Remembering God's help to the nation in the past
and pleading for God's help in the present

1   We have heard by word of mouth, O God,
    stories passed on to us from our ancestors,
    of your deeds in their time long ago.

2   How you settled them in the land,
    after driving out other nations,
    how you crushed other peoples,
    but helped them grow and flourish.

3   For they did not take possession of any land
    through their own weapons,
    or win victory by their own hand.
    It was solely by your arm and your right hand—
    for you looked with favor on them.

4   Now you are our King and our God—
    you can command that Jacob's heirs be set free.

5	It is through you that we could topple our enemies,
	through your name that we could trample them underfoot.
6	Arming ourselves will not save us—
	trusting in weapons will not bring victory.
7	For it was you who saved us from our enemies
	and put to shame those who hated us.
8	God, in you we boast all day long,
	and give you thanks continually.
9	Except now you have rejected us and shamed us.
	You have not gone out with our armies.
10	So we turned and ran from the enemy,
	and they ransacked us.
11	You left us to be devoured like sheep,
	and scattered us among the nations.
12	You sold your own people for a trifle,
	demanding next to nothing for them.
13	You made us the taunt of our neighbors,
	the derision and scorn of those around us.
14	You made us a joke among the nations,
	a laughingstock among the peoples.
15, 16	All day long our disgrace parades before us,
	and we are too ashamed to show our faces,
	because they are pointed out by those who taunt and mock us,
	in sight of the enemy and avenger.
17	While all of this came upon us
	we did not forget you,
	or renege on our side of the covenant.
18	Our steps have not deviated from your way,
	and neither have our hearts forsaken you.
19	Yet you have broken us like wild animals their prey,
	and left us in the darkness of death.

| 20, 21 | You, O God, would soon discover
if we had forgotten you and turned to worship other gods,
for you know the inner secrets of the heart. |
|---|---|
| 22 | But because you have forsaken us,
we are being killed daily,
being regarded as sheep for the slaughter. |
| 23 | Wake up to our plight!
Do not go on sleeping!
Ignore us no longer! |
| 24 | Why are you turning your back on us?
Why do you ignore our oppression and suffering? |
| 25 | For we have fallen right into the dirt,
lying prone in the dust of the earth. |
| 26 | Arouse yourself and help us!
In your loving kindness come and save us! |

Psalm 45

A royal psalm—a wedding song for the king

| 1 | My heart is full of good thoughts
that overflow into a praise-poem for the king,
my tongue being the pen of the praise-singer. |
|---|---|
| 2 | You are the most striking-looking of men.
Grace is poured onto your lips,
and God has blessed you forever. |
| 3 | Buckle your sword to your thigh,
clothe yourself in splendor and majesty. |
| 4 | Ride on victoriously in your splendor,
willing to defend what is true and right,
your right hand displaying awesome power. |

PSALM 45

5   Your arrows are sharp, piercing the heart of the enemy,
so that the people fall into line.

6   Your throne is like God's throne,
enduring for ever and ever.
Your royal scepter is one of justice.

7   You love justice and hate wickedness,
therefore God, your God,
has chosen you above your fellows,
and anointed you
with the oil of gladness.

8   Your robes are full of the fragrance
of myrrh and aloes and cassia.
The air resounds with the glad music
of stringed instruments.

9   Surrounding you are the daughters of kings
as your ladies of honor.
Your queen, wearing gold from Ophir,
stands at your right hand.

10   Listen to this, O princess,
bride-to-be, and take it all in.
Forget your people and your father's house,

11   The king is now your Lord—
pay him honor
and he will desire you.

12   You will also be showered with gifts—
from the richest of people
and the most unexpected.
Then they will entreat your favor.

13   Listen, O king, the princess is dressed
ready in her quarters.
Her dress is decorated with gold
and colorful embroidery.

| 14 | She will come to you
with her young women attendants. |
|---|---|
| 15 | They will come in joy,
rejoicing as they enter the king's palace. |
| 16 | In place of your parents,
there will be children filling your house,
who will become rulers worldwide. |
| 17 | God promises that the king's name
will be remembered for all generations.
Already now the people praise him
and shall do so forever. |

Psalm 46

*A national hymn of thanksgiving after victory in a battle—
a mighty fortress is our God*

| 1 | God is our shelter and our strength,
always there to help us when in trouble—
we shall not be afraid. |
|---|---|
| 2, 3 | Though the foundations of the earth itself be shaken,
we shall not be afraid.
Though the mountains rise up out of the sea, cracking and shifting,
we shall not be afraid.
Though the sea roars and rages in tumult,
we shall not be afraid. |
| 4, 5 | In the city where our God, the God above all, dwells,
streams flow to bring it joy,
and God is there among the people of God,
ready to help at the first opportunity. |
| 6 | If God, the one in charge, utters a word
the earth could melt,
and chaos reign among its people. |

| 7 | *But the Lord Almighty,*
the God of Jacob and Rachel, is with us.
This same God is our shelter and our strength. |
|---|---|
| 8 | Look and see what the Lord has done—
devastated the war-mongering nations. |
| 9,10 | God, whose voice can be heard above the tumult,
has declared that wars should cease.
"I will destroy all weapons,
breaking them, smashing them, burning them.
Be still and know that I am God.
I am the one who will be praised and worshipped,
by believer and nonbeliever alike,
throughout the world." |
| 11 | *The Lord Almighty,*
the God of Jacob and Rachel, is with us.
This same God is our shelter and our strength. |

Psalm 47

Praise to God as King in a song of triumph

| 1 | Clap your hands, all you people!
Sing to God loud songs of joy! |
|---|---|
| 2 | For our Lord, the God above all, is awesome,
ruling over the whole world. |
| 3 | He helped us triumph over the nations around us
and become their rulers. |
| 4 | God chose this land for us.
It has become the pride of his beloved Jacob and Rachel. |
| 5 | God went up with a shout—
he ascended with a blast of the trumpet. |

6	Sing hymns to our God, sing hymns. Sing praises to our King, sing praises.
7	For God is the King of the whole world. Sing songs, sing psalms of praise.
8	God reigns over his people, the people of Abraham and Sarah, but also, over those who do not acknowledge him.
9	Gather together, and lift God high in song and praise. God reigns high over all!

Psalm 48

In praise of the city of Zion (Jerusalem) and God's presence there

1	Great is the Lord! God's glory is praised in this city, high on its holy mountain, Mount Zion.
2, 3	Its beauty is celebrated world-wide— the city of the great king. Set high on the north side, it is strongly defended by God.
4	The kings assembled together, and came to attack Mount Zion,
5	But when they saw it they were amazed— and panic-stricken.
6, 7	They were filled with fear as a woman is when labor pains first start, as sailors are when an east wind threatens to smash their ships sailing out of Tarshish. They fled!
8	We have heard about this and have also seen for ourselves, in the city of the Lord of all creation, in the city of our God, the city in which God will reign forever.

9	On our part, O God, we contemplate your constant love within your temple.
10	Your name has spread world-wide, and so has praise of you and of your goodness.
11	All in Mount Zion, and in all the towns of Judah, rejoice at your judgements.
12	Walk around Mount Zion, count its towers, inspect its walls,
13	Take a good look at its defenses so that you can tell the next generation that this is all the doing of God, our God,
14	And this same God will be our God till the end of time. Yes, God will be our guide for ever and ever.

Psalm 49

A teaching psalm, pondering the meaning of life and death

1	Listen, everyone, open your ears, all of you.
2	Each one should hear this, high-born and low, rich and poor.
3, 4	Now I am going to speak words of wisdom, accompanied with my lyre, about the meaning of proverbs and the solution to riddles, because I have thought long in my heart, looking for understanding.
5	Why should I be fearful in evil days, when persecution snaps at my heels?

6	The wealthy try to use their wealth to save them,
7	But can they ultimately redeem their brother? Can they pay God the ransom for their sister?
8, 9	It costs more than this to redeem another's soul, and one can never rescue another from the grave.
10	Everyone dies, the wise and the foolish alike, and their wealth is left to others.
11	They may think that their family name and legacy will last down the generations, even naming their estates with their own names.
12	But no human being can live forever—they all die, just as the animals do.
13	Such is the fate of the foolish, and of those who were pleased with themselves.
14	Like sheep they are bound for the grave, shepherded by death. They will descend straight to Sheol which will be their home.
15	But God will ransom my life from the power of the grave, and will take me in.
16	Do not be envious when someone becomes rich, and their estate increases in wealth.
17	When they die they can take none of it with them— every last cent stays behind.
18	While they lived, they might have been pleased with themselves, and even had the praise of others.
19	But when they go to join their ancestors there will be no spotlight to shine on them.
20	For no human being can live forever—they all die, just as the animals do.

Psalm 50

The judgement of God, the God above all other gods

1   The mighty God, the Lord, speaks the word,
waking the earth,
from the rising of the sun to its setting.

2   God's light radiates out of Zion—
beauty in perfection.

3   Our God is coming and not in silence—
fire goes before him and hurricanes swirl around him.

4   He calls from the heavens above and the earth below,
in order to judge his people.

5   "Gather together all those faithful to me,
those who have sacrificed to make a covenant with me."

6   The heavens will declare his righteousness in all things,
for God himself is the judge.

7   "Listen, all my people," he cries out,
"for I am speaking to you.
Hear me, O Israel—for I am God, your God.
My judgement is against you.

8   My complaint against you is not because of your sacrifices—
you make enough of those.

9   I will not ask for a bull from your pen,
nor a goat from your fold.

10   For every creature in the forest is mine.
I own the cattle on a thousand hills,

11   I know every bird from here to the mountains,
and every creature in the wild belongs to me.

12   If I were hungry, I would not tell you.
I own the whole world and everything in it.

13   Do I in any case eat the flesh of bulls
and drink goat's blood?

14	Rather offer me your thanksgiving, and fulfil the vows you make to me, the God above all others.
15	Then, when you call on me in times of trouble, I will come and rescue you, and you will bring glory to me.
16–18	Here is God's word to the wayward, 'You hate my discipline and take no heed to my words. You make friends with thieves and rapists— what right have you to piously recite my commands and espouse my covenant?
19	Your mouth is given over to evil and your tongue offers only deceit.
20	You bad-mouth your own brothers, and you slander your own sisters.
21	These are the kinds of things you do, and you think I accept this kind of behavior because I say nothing in response? I do not! I detest it! and will set things right before your very eyes.
22	Put these things foremost in your thoughts, those who want to forget me, before I rip you apart, with no one to come to your aid.
23	It is those who offer a sacrifice of thanksgiving to honor me, and those who order their lives aright, that I will save'."

Psalm 51

*A prayer of contrition traditionally attributed to David,
after Nathan the prophet made him aware of his guilt in committing
adultery with Bathsheba, but probably written centuries later.*

1. Have mercy on me, O God,
   in keeping with your constant love.
   Wipe out all my wrongdoings,
   in keeping with your copious mercy.

2. Thoroughly wash away my iniquity,
   and wipe away all my sin.

3. For I know too well where I have gone wrong.
   My leaning towards evil confronts me all the time.

4. It is against you that I have done wrong—you alone.
   You are right to judge me, and your sentence is just.

5. For in fact, I have been in the wrong
   since my mother conceived me,
   and a sinner since I was born.

6. I am aware that you want truth from deep within—
   in those secret places, teach me wisdom.

7. Deep-clean me to make me pure,
   scrub me to make me whiter than snow.

8. Let my broken parts rejoice again.
   Enable me to experience joy and gladness.

9. Look no longer at my sins,
   and wipe out every evil that is part of me.

10. Renew me! Give me a pure heart
    and the right spirit within.

11. Do not ban me from your presence,
    and do not take your Holy Spirit from me.

12. Give me back the joy I had
    when first you set me free,
    and strengthen me with the gift of your spirit.

13   Then I will teach other sinners your ways,
      so that they too may turn back to you.

14   O God my savior, save me
      from having to pay with my own blood.
      Then my tongue will sing songs of your generosity.

15   O Lord—open my lips
      and my mouth will tell out your praise.

16   Making a sacrifice before you does not please you—
      bringing a burnt offering, gives you no delight.

17   The sacrifice you really want
      is the sacrifice of a broken spirit—
      a broken and a crushed heart you will not reject.

18*   Be pleased to rebuild the walls of Jerusalem,
      and be good to Zion.

19   Then the right sacrifices will delight you—
      bulls offered on your altar.

Psalm 52

*The one who destroys others will be destroyed,
the one who trusts in God will flourish*

1   You who are great in the eyes of the world,
      why do you boast of destroying the faithful?

2   For day by day you plan destruction—
      your tongue razor-sharp, your mouth deceit.

3   You love evil before good,
      to lie rather than to speak the truth.

---

* Verses 18 and 19 are most probably a later addition.

Psalm 53

4   You love all words that dishonor,
        O deceitful tongue.

5   God will destroy you utterly in the same way,
        plucking you out of your home,
        banishing you from the land of the living.

6   Good people will see,
        be warned, and deride you, saying,

7   "This is the one who turned from God as his strength,
        who trusted in the size of his wealth,
        and in consolidating his evil ways."

8   But I am like a green olive tree
        that flourishes in God's house,
        for I put my trust in the constant love of God.

9   I will praise you forever for your good deeds.
        Together with all the faithful I will hope in your name,
        for it is goodness itself.

Psalm 53[*]

Fools believe there is no God: not one of them does good

1   Fools believe in their hearts that there is no God.
        They are rotten to the core,
        as their abominable actions show.
        Not one of them does good.

2   God looks out upon the whole of humankind
        to see if there are any who try to understand,
        any who seek him.

3   They have all turned away.
        They are all equally evil.
        There is no-one who does any good—

---

[*] Psalm 53 is the same as Psalm 14, with the exception of a few words and Yahweh (Lord) is used there, while El (God) is used here. They have been rendered differently.

	not even one.
4	Do they know nothing, those evildoers, who eat up my people as they eat bread? They never call upon God.
5	Then when the enemy attacks they are helpless with terror. They have no need to be, because God scatters the enemy, and puts the God-deniers to shame.
6	O that the salvation of Israel would come from Zion. When God leads all the people back, then Jacob will be glad, Israel will rejoice.

Psalm 54

A royal prayer for deliverance from foreign enemies

1	Save me, O God, by your name— set me free by your power.
2	Listen to my prayer, O God, give ear to the words of my mouth.
3	For strangers have turned against me, and oppressors seek my life. They do not see you there backing me up.
4	But I know for sure, that you, O God, are my helper. You are the one who guards my life.
5	You will repay my enemies for their evil. In your faithfulness you will end their power.
6	O God, I will freely make sacrifices for you, giving thanks to your name, for it is good.

| 7 | For you have pulled me out of every trouble,
and I have looked down victorious on my enemies. |

Psalm 55

The lament of an individual over the open hostility of fellow citizens, and especially over the betrayal of a friend

| 1 | Bend your ear to my prayer, O Lord.
Do not ignore my request. |
| 2 | Turn to me and give me an answer.
I am distraught |
| 3 | Because of the noisy clamor of the enemy—
those who hate me and wish to do me harm. |
| 4 | I am heart-sore and full of terror,
fearful of death, overwhelmed by horror. |
| 5–8 | I say to myself, "If only I had wings like a dove,
I would fly away as quickly as I could
and find refuge.
I would settle far away from here in the wilderness,
where I would find shelter
from the raging wind and storm." |
| 9–11 | O Lord, confound the enemy's propaganda—
it brings violence and strife into the city,
as day and night, they send it out into the streets.
Now trouble and suffering eat away at its center,
corruption and fraud at its marketplace. |
| 12 | But it is not the enemy out there who taunts me,
that I could bear.
It is not opponents who treat me insolently,
I could avoid them, |
| 13 | But you, my equal, my companion,
my dear friend. |

14 We enjoyed each other's company,
and worshipped together in God's house,
mingling with the crowds.

15 Let death come upon all my enemies
and drag them down to Sheol,
for both their homes and their hearts
are full of venom.

16 As for me,
I called upon God,
and the Lord saved me.

17 Morning, evening and at noon, I prayed,
groaning and crying before God.

18 God heard my cry,
making payment for my life,
drawing near to me when so many were against me,
and restoring my peace.

19 God is on the throne from ages past,
the same through all of time.
The enemy rejects this and has no fear of God.

20 When we were at peace,
my erstwhile friend broke his covenant
by attacking his closest ally.

21 His speech was soft as butter,
his heart set on war.
His words were smooth as oil
yet sharp as a drawn sword.

22 Bring your burdens to the Lord—
he will bear you up.
He never allows the righteous to be shaken.

23 And the Lord will not allow
the blood-thirsty and treacherous
to live out even half their days
before they are thrown into

the pit of destruction.
For my part, I will always trust in the Lord.

Psalm 56

What can people do to me if I trust in God?

1   Be gracious to me, O God,
for my enemy tramples all over me.

2   All day long they hold me down—
and there are so many fighting against me.

3   O God above all others,
when I am afraid, I put my trust in you.
I praise your word.

4   When I trust in you and am not afraid,
what can people do to me?

5   Every day the enemy twists my words.
They are always plotting against me
in some evil way.

6, 7   They conspire together secretly,
spying on me, wanting my very life.
Do they think they can get away with it?
Pour your anger on these people,
and bring them down, O God.

8   Count each time I complain.
Collect all my tears in a bottle—
record them in your book.

9   My enemy will turn back in defeat,
for I call out to you, and I am sure of this—
God is on my side.

10, 11   It is in God whose word I praise,
in the Lord whose word I praise,
that I trust, and I am not afraid,
for what can humans do to me?

12   I will indeed pay my vows to you, O God,
along with offerings of thanks.

13   For you have delivered my soul from death,
and my feet from tripping up.
Now I can walk before you,
in the light of life.

Psalm 57

*A prayer of thanksgiving for being rescued
after taking shelter with God.*

1   Be merciful to me, O God, be merciful.
I put my life in your hands,
for my soul finds refuge in you.
I will take refuge under the shelter of your wings
till the raging storms pass by.

2   I cry to God, the supreme God,
because you, O God, are working out
your purpose for me.

3   I know you will reach out from heaven to save me,
and turn the tables on those
whose aim is to crush me.
You will enfold me
in your steadfast love and mercy.

4   I lie down among those who encircle me
like lions, their teeth spears
and their tongues sharp swords.

5   *Be raised high above us, O God,*
         so that your glory fills the whole universe.

6   My soul reached a low point when
         they set a net in my way—
         when they dug a deep pit in my path.
         But they fell into it themselves.

7   This restored my soul,
         and made me want to sing
         and give praise to you, O God.

8, 9*   It sang out,
         "Wake up, soul!
         Wake up, lyre and harp!"
         I will wake early and sing praises to you
         among the people,
         among all the people on earth.

10   For your mercy is as high as the heavens,
         your truth stretching far beyond the clouds.

11   O Lord, may you be held in honor
         higher than the heavens,
         and lifted up in glory
         far above the earth.

Psalm 58**

Revenge is sweet—exalting over violent retribution for the wicked

1   Do you rule justly, you warlords?
         Do you govern the people fairly?

2   No! For in your hearts you are plotting evil,
         and your hands direct violence on earth.

---

   * Verses 8–11 are found again in Ps 108:1–5, although this version is worded differently.

   ** Psalm 58 contains some of the most difficult phrases in the Psalter. (vss 4–10). The Hebrew text of this is badly damaged, so much of the translation is conjecture.

3	The wicked go astray from the womb, take the wrong path from their birth.
4	They hiss out venom like a snake, mouthing lies— like a deaf adder they plug their ears,
5	So that they do not hear the voice of the charmer, no matter how alluring their enchantment.
6	O God, restore justice—break their teeth in their mouths. Shatter the jaws of the young lions.
7	Let them drain away like continuously running water, be trodden down and wither like grass.
8	Let them be like the slug that dissolves into slime, like a premature birth that never lives to see the sun.
9	Let them be like a batch of pots that is swept away before the branches of the thorn tree are brought to fire them.
10	When they see retribution like this, the righteous will rejoice. They will wash their feet in the blood of the wicked.
11	They will say, "There is truly a reward for the right-living person. There is truly a God who judges justly on earth."

Psalm 59

A plea for delivery from enemies, and punishment for them

1	Deliver me from my enemies, O my God. Protect me from those working against me.
2	Save me from evildoers, and deliver me from the bloodthirsty.
3	Look! They are waiting for me. They are agitating to take my life, and not from any fault of mine.

PSALM 59

4   They are preparing to attack me,
    and not from any sin I have committed.
    Look and see, Lord God Almighty.

5   Lord God of Israel,
    get up and punish all the non-believers.
    Spare none of those who plot evil.

6   Each evening they are back,
    prowling through the city
    and baying like dogs.

7   They spit out threats,
    their words, sharp as daggers—
    all the while thinking,
    "Who is there to hear us?"

8   But you are listening,
    laughing at them,
    holding them in derision.

9   And that is why, O God, I wait for you.
    You are my defense—
    you are my strength and my fortress.

10 O God of mercy, you will save me.
    You will let me triumph over my enemies.

11 Do not wipe them out completely, God—
    lest the people forget.
    Make them totter and fall,

12 For the evil that came out of their mouths,
    for the twisted words from their haughty lips,
    and for their cursing and lying.

13 Consume them in your anger
    so that they are no more.
    Then it will be acknowledged
    throughout the world
    that God rules over the children
    of Jacob and Rachel.

14 But then each evening,
    send them back,

	prowling through the city
	howling like dogs,
15	This time looking for food,
	and growling from hunger.
16	But I will sing of your power –
	I will sing from break of day
	of your constant love—
	of your protection and refuge
	while I was in trouble.
17	O God of strength and mercy,
	you are my fortress,
	and I will sing praises
	to your constant love.

Psalm 60

A national lament and prayer that God would free those he loves

1	O, God, you have rejected us,
	been angry with us and left us in disarray.
	Turn again to help us.
2	You have sent earthquakes tearing open the land.
	Come and mend the cracks, for it is still trembling.
3	You have left us to suffer greatly.
	The wine you gave us to drink has made us reel.
4	Yet you have given some token to those who worship you,
	a banner of truth to display—
5	Come, set free those you love,
	and give them victory with your right hand.
6*	God has spoken in his holiness,
	"Gladly will I divide up Shechem,
	and share out the valley of Succoth.

* Verses 6–12 are the same as Ps 108:7–13, although this version is worded differently.

7   Gilead belongs to me, as does Manasseh.
    Ephraim is my helmet, Judah my scepter.

8   Moab is my washbasin.
    On Edom I fling my sandal.
    Over Philistia I exult in triumph."

9   Who is going to lead us into the fortified city?
    Who will lead us into Edom?

10 Will you, O God?
    Or have you indeed rejected us,
    because you no longer go out with our army?

11 Give us your help against the enemy—
    it is hopeless relying on other people.

12 But with your help, O God, we will do valiantly,
    for you will trample down our enemies.

Psalm 61

A plea for help to God as rock and mother bird—a royal prayer.

1   Hear my cry, O God!
    Listen to my prayer.

2   I am at the end of my tether,
    my heart being overwhelmed,
    as I cry to you to lead me to a rock
    high above me.

3   For you offer shelter from the enemy,
    like a strong tower.

4   O God, let me stay in your house forever,
    nestling under the shelter of your wings.

5   For you have heard my plea—
    you have put me in line for the heritage
    of those who worship you.

6   Prolong the life of the king.
    May his life endure as the generations pass.

7   May he be enthroned for ever before you,
   secure in your constant love and faithfulness.

8   So I will sing your praises, day after day
   as I come to renew my commitment to you.

Psalm 62

God alone is my rock and fortress, my hope, and my salvation

1   Only in God is my being quiet.
   Only in God do I find salvation.

2   God alone is my rock and fortress—
   and my salvation.
   I shall never be shaken.

3   How long will those with evil in their hearts
   go on attacking others,
   battering them as they would
   a leaning wall or a rickety fence?

4   They have one plan—
   to bring down those of high esteem.
   They take delight in lies,
   uttering blessings with their mouths
   while inwardly cursing.

5   Only in God is my being quiet.
   Only in God is my hope.

6   He alone is my rock and fortress—
   I shall never be shaken,

7   For in God is not only my salvation and my glory,
   but my strength and my shelter.

8   All of you—trust in God at all times—
   pour out your hearts before the one
   who will take care of you.

9   Look at other people—
    if they are lowly born
    they are light as a breath,
    high-born, but a delusion.
    Neither make any impact on the scales.

10 It is a vain hope to think
    that you could gain anything
    through extortion or theft.
    And if you do acquire riches
    do not be enamored of them,

11 I heard this word of God once—
    and I heard it repeated.
    All power belongs to God,
    as does loving kindness.
    God repays each person
    in accordance with their actions.

Psalm 63

Longing for and meditating on God

1   O God, my God, I search for you.
    My flesh longs for you.
    My soul thirsts for you,
    as a dry and parched land longs for water.

2   For I have seen your power and your glory
    in the sanctuary.

3   Your constant love is far better
    than the life and lips that praise you.

4   With hands lifted up I will bless you,
    and call on your name,
    as long as I live.

5   My soul is satisfied as with the richest of fare,
    and my lips joyfully praise you,

6	My mind turns to you while I am in bed,
	and I meditate on you in the small hours,
7	Remembering how you helped me
	and held me up high.
8	So my soul clings to you and rejoices
	under the shadow of your wings.
9	Those who try to destroy my life
	will end up in earth's lowest depths—
10	Meeting their end through violence
	and becoming food for jackals.
10	Lying mouths will be plugged,
	but the king and those
	who give him their allegiance
	will rejoice in God.

Psalm 64

A description of evil people, a prayer to have no fear of them, with an assurance that God is in charge

1	Listen to my complaint to you, O God—
	free me from fear of the enemy.
2	Hide me from the plots of the wicked,
	from the under-hand scheming
	of those bent on wrongdoing.
3	They sharpen their tongues like knives,
	and shoot venomous words like arrows.
4	They lie in ambush to shoot at the innocent,
	attacking suddenly,
	without fearing the consequences.
5	They encourage each other
	in secretly pursuing their evil goals,
	all the while thinking, "Who is watching?"

| 6 | They search deep into their hearts and minds
for even more evil ways to snare their victims—
and the human heart is deep indeed. |
| --- | --- |
| 7 | But suddenly they are the ones who will be wounded,
for you, God will shoot your arrows at them. |
| 8 | You will turn their own tongues on them,
and everyone will avoid them, trembling in fear. |
| 9 | Fear will fall on everyone,
and they will talk about what you have done,
and think deeply about your actions. |
| 10 | Those whose lives are good and true
will rejoice in you, Lord—
they will trust in you and give you the glory. |

Psalm 65

Praise to the God of the harvest

| 1 | Praise is waiting for you in Zion, O God,
and vows will be paid in your presence. |
| --- | --- |
| 2 | The whole of humankind will come before you,
the one who listens to our prayers. |
| 3 | We will bring to you our sins beyond counting,
and ask you for forgiveness. |
| 4 | Blessed indeed are those you choose
and enable to get close to you—
to enter your courts.
They will be imbued with the beauty of your house,
the holiness of your temple. |
| 5, 6 | You answer us with acts of awesome power,
O God of our salvation.
You give hope to those at the ends of the earth,
confidence to those at sea,
for you made the mountains
that encircle the sea with power. |

	You stilled the noise of its chaos,
	of waves roaring and people in tumult.
7	These were signs that struck fear
	into the hearts of those
	who lived at earth's furthest bounds.
8	You also made the morning,
	which opens its gates each day,
	and shuts them again
	each evening with rejoicing.
9	You visit the earth and water it,
	enriching it with water from the river of God.
	You provide the earth with grain as was your plan.
10	You drench the ridges of the hills,
	and the hollows of the valleys,
	making them soft with the falling rain,
	and causing fresh growth.
11	You crown the year with plenty—
	your carts carry in
	an abundant harvest.
12	The hills of the wilderness rejoice all around,
	their pastures dotted with flocks,
	their valleys decked with grain.
	They sing—they shout for joy!

Psalm 66

Praise God, all people on earth, for his awesome deeds

1	Praise God with a joyful noise,
	all people on earth!
2	Sing out in God's honor!
	Praise the glory of his name!

Psalm 66

3   Tell God how his actions fill you with awe—
       that even his enemies bow down before him.

4   O God, all on earth will worship you,
       and sing praises to your name.

5   Come and see what God has done!
       How awesome are his deeds
       among the children of the earth.

6   He turned water into dry land,
       enabling our ancestors
       to walk through the sea on foot.
       How we rejoiced in God then.

7   The God who rules forever by his might,
       keeps his eye on every nation,
       in case the rebellious get above themselves.

8   O bless our God, all you people,
       so that the sound of his praise is heard far and wide.

9   O God, you kept our soul alive
       and our feet from slipping.

10   For you have tested us—
       you have tried us as silver is tried.

11   You trapped us in the net,
       laid heavy loads upon our backs,

12   You let other people ride rough-shod over us,
       leading us through fire and water,
       till you brought us out into this rich place.

13   I will come into your house with my offerings,
       I will fulfil the promises I made to you.

14   The vows I swore when I was in trouble,
       the promises I cried aloud to you,
       when I was in great distress.

15   As the incense rises in worship,
       I will give of my all to you,
       in both practical and spiritual giving.

16   I will invite all those who worship God
to come and hear what he has done for me.

17   While my mouth cried out loud to him for help,
my tongue also extolled him.

18, 19   If I had cherished any thoughts
of wrongdoing in my heart,
the Lord would not have listened,
but he did hear every word of my prayer.

20   Blessed be God
who did not turn his listening ear away,
nor his mercy and care for me.

Psalm 67

Calling all people to praise God

1   O God, be gracious and merciful to us.
Smile upon us,

2   So that everyone on earth may know your way,
all peoples your power to save.

3   *May all the people praise you, O God,*
May all the people praise you.

4   May all nations be glad
and full of joyous song,
for your judgement is unbiased
and your governance true.

5   *May all the people praise you, O God,*
May all the people praise you.

6   Then the earth will yield her bounty,
and God, our own God, will bless us abundantly.

7   Yes, God will bless us,
and everyone will worship this same God
to the very ends of the earth.

Psalm 68

Celebration of the way God led the Israelites out of Egypt and into the land of Canaan, and a call on all people on earth to praise God. One of the older psalms

1	May God arise and scatter every enemy. May those who hate God flee.
2	As smoke is dispersed by wind, may they be dispersed. As wax melts before the fire, may the wicked perish before God.
3	But may those doing right be joyful. may they be ecstatic with joy. may they exult before God.
4	We will all sing to you, God, sing praises to you, extol the one who rides on the clouds – magnify you by your name, Yahweh, rejoicing before you.
5	You, God, who dwell in holiness, are parent to orphans, and defender of widows.
6	You give families to those who are alone, unshackling those bound with chains, but leaving the rebellious in a dry land.
7	O God, when you went in front, leading our people, when you journeyed with us through the wilderness,
8	The earth shook and the heavens unleashed torrents of rain, at your presence, O God, the God of Israel.
9	You sent rain and in plenty,

PSALM 68

      confirming the heritage you gave to your people
      when they started to doubt.

10   It became the home of the faithful,
      the place you prepared for the needy.

11   You, Lord, gave your word.
      It was spread abroad
      by a great company of people.

12   Armies led by their kings all fled,
      and the women at home divided the spoils.

13   Though you are covered in black soot
      like a pot in the fire,
      you will be like a dove
      made with wings covered in silver,
      and feathers tipped with gold.

14   Mount Salmon was white with snow when
      the Lord Almighty scattered kings there.

15   O Bashan, a mighty mountain,
      a mountain of many peaks,
      why do you think the Lord should
      dwell on your heights?

16   God has chosen this high hill as home,
      and will live here forever,.

17   The Lord is the same God, the God of Sinai,
      coming to this holy place.
      as head of an army of twenty thousand chariots,
      and thousands of angels.

18   God ascended to the heights,
      leading the captors captive,
      with the tributes of the people—
      even those of the rebels.

19   Blessed be the Lord,
      the God of our salvation,
      who day by day pours blessings on us.

20   Our God is indeed a God who saves,
      who controls both life and death.

Psalm 68

21	God will wound the heads of all enemies,
	split the skulls of the wrongdoers.
22	God said, "I will bring my people from Bashan,
	and from the depths of the sea,
23	That the blood of the enemy flow at your feet
	and your dogs wet their tongues with it."
24	The processions have come into view, O God,
	the processions of God our King,
	going into the sanctuary.
25	Led by the singers,
	with the musicians following,
	and among them, young women playing tambourines.
26	They sing, "Bless God in the congregation,
	bless the Lord, the fountain of Israel."
27	In the lead is Benjamin the smallest,
	and their leader,
	together with the princes of Judah,
	the princes of Zebulun and those of Naphtali.
28, 29	You have been our strength in the past, O God.
	Show your might and strengthen us again
	from your temple in Jerusalem.
	May kings bring gifts to you.
30	Rebuke the people who act
	like wild animals among the reeds,
	like bulls harrowing the calves.
	Subdue those that lust after tributes of silver.
	Scatter those nations that delight in war.
31	May princes come from Egypt—
	from Ethiopia let them come
	to worship God.
32	All kingdoms on earth,
	Sing to God,

Sing Praises!

33 Listen to the one who rides through the heavens,
the ancient heavens.
Listen to God's commanding voice.

34 Acknowledge that power belongs to God,
whose majesty and power stretch
from Israel to the stars.

35 O God, you are awesome in your sanctuary.
You give power and strength to your people.
Blessed be God!

Psalm 69

*Lament of an individual who is being mocked and attacked,
asking to be rescued*

1 Save me, O God,
for I am in water up to my neck.

2 I am sinking into the sludge
where I find no foothold,
and as the waters deepen,
they sweep over me in floods.

3 I am exhausted from crying—
it has parched my throat.
Tears have blurred my sight,
as I watch for you, my God.

4 So many hate me without cause,
more than the number of hairs on my head.
They want to destroy me,
by accusing me falsely,
demanding I return what I took—
but I took nothing!

Psalm 69

5   Lord, I have been foolish,
    and you know it,
    I have done wrong,
    and you have seen it plainly.

6   Lord God Almighty,
    do not let those who wait on you
    be ashamed because of me.
    Do not let those who seek you
    be confused because of me.

7   I have been reproached on your behalf,
    and been shamed to my face for your sake.

8   I have become a stranger to my family,
    an alien to my siblings.

9   It is zeal for your cause
    that has fired me up,
    and the accusations against you
    have been turned on me.

10 When I wept and fasted
    I was insulted.

11 When I put on the garments of mourning,
    I became the focus of mockery.

12 I am mocked by the elite
    and even figure in the drinking songs of the day.

13 Yet, despite all this,
    I keep on praying to you, O Lord.
    In your good time,
    in your abundant love and mercy,
    answer me by rescuing me.

14 Pull me out of the mud,
    stop me from sinking,
    and from being submerged in floodwater.
    Deliver me from those who hate me.

15	Do not allow the waters to swallow me up,
	or the pit to close its mouth on me.
16	Answer me, O Lord,
	in the goodness of your constant love to me,
	in the abundance of your mercy.
17	Do not hide your face from your servant,
	but be quick to answer me,
	for I am in trouble.
18	Draw near to me. Redeem me.
	Deliver me from my enemies.
19	You know the slander I receive,
	my shame and my dishonor—
	my attackers are all known to you.
20	The slander has broken my heart—
	it weighs me down.
	I looked for some to take my side,
	but there was no-one,
	some to offer comfort,
	there was not one.
21	They gave me bitter food to eat,
	and for my thirst gave me vinegar to drink.
22	May they be forced to eat
	what they would give to others.
	May they be snared in their own traps.
23	May their eyes be dulled so they cannot see
	and their limbs continually shake.
24	Pour out your indignation onto them,
	and may your burning anger
	have its way with them,
25	So that their houses become derelict
	and their dwellings uninhabited.
26	They attack the ones you are already punishing,
	and add to the grief of those already suffering.

PSALM 69

27 Add guilt to their guilt
    with no acquittal for them.

28 Blot out their names from the book of life.
    Never write them in with the righteous.

29 But I am full of sorrow and distress.
    Rescue me, protect me.

30 I will sing praises to you, O God,
    exalting your name in a song of thanksgiving.

31 This will please you more
    than the sacrifice of hoofed animals,
    of ox or of bull.

32 Let those who are suffering like me,
    those who are searching for God,
    see it and take heart,

33 For the Lord does listen to those in bondage,
    or who possess very little.

34 May all the earth and heaven praise God,
    the seas, as well as all living creatures.

35 For God will restore Zion
    and the cities of Judah,
    so that the people of God may return
    and possess them once again.

36 It will pass to their progeny as an inheritance,
    and those who love God's name will live in it.

Psalm 70*

Come quickly to my aid, O Lord.

1   Come quickly, O God, to rescue me,
        Come quickly to help me, O Lord.

2   But those who are out to get me,
        who are after my very life—
        may they be confounded and disgraced—
        may they be stopped in their tracks
        and turned right around.

3   May those who crow about their victory
        be thrown into confusion instead.

4   But may those who desire to follow you
        find their happiness in you,
        and may those who love your saving grace
        be able to say continuously
        "God is great!"

4   I am weak and always in need of you.
        Come to me without delay.
        You are my helper and my rescuer.
        Come as quickly as you can.

Psalm 71

*An individual pleads, in old age, for deliverance from enemies,
with thanks for help in his youth*

1   In you, O Lord, I have found refuge.
        Let me never be put to shame.

---

* The words of Ps 70, with a few differences, are the same as Ps 40:13–17. I have rendered them differently.

Psalm 71

2 Turn your ear my way,
   and in your way,
   the right way, set me free.

3 You are my rock and my fortress—
   be the fortress that keeps me safe,
   the rock where I find refuge.

4 Rescue me, O God, from the clutches of the wicked,
   from the grasp of those who are crooked and cruel.

5 For I have put my hope in you, O Lord God,
   I have trusted in you since my youth.

6 You have kept me steady since you gave me birth,
   ever since I was in my mother's womb.
   I praise you continually.

7 Many look askance at me, but you are my strong refuge.

8 Keep me praising you and honoring you all day long.

9 When I am old, do not cast me aside—
   do not ignore me when my strength is spent.

10 For my enemies spread rumors against me,
   conspiring together and lying in wait
   to take my very life.

11 They say, "God has forgotten him.
   Go after him—attack him,
   for no-one will come to his aid."

12 O, my God, do not leave me.
   Come quickly to help me.

13 Let those against me be consumed by shame,
   those who wish me harm
   be covered with scorn and disgrace.

14 Still I will go on in hope,
   and praise you more and more.

15 All day long my voice will tell
   of your righteous acts and your saving deeds,
   though they are too numerous to count.

16 I will go on in your strength, O my Lord God,
    and talk only of your righteousness.

17 O God, you taught me when I was young,
    and since then, I have told others
    of your wonderful deeds.

18 It is the same now I am old, and my hair is grey.
    O God, do not abandon me,
    not until I have shown your strength
    to this generation
    and your power to the next.

19 For your righteousness is the highest,
    and your creation the greatest, O God.
    Who can compare with you?

20 You, the very one who led me into such suffering,
    will revive me again,
    and lift me up from the depths.

21 You will restore my good reputation,
    and comfort me in every way.

22 Then I will sing songs of praise to you, O God
    on stringed instruments,
    extolling your faithfulness, O Holy One.

23 My body and soul will be lifted high
    in singing praises to you,
    the one who rescued me.

24 My enemies are vanquished—
    and I will never tire
    of telling others about this.

Psalm 72*

*A prayer for the king, which paints a picture of a model king.
One of the oldest of the psalms*

1   Endow the king with good judgement, O God,
       teach him what is right.

2   Then he will judge your people with justice,
       and the poor with an even hand,

3   So that the mountains themselves
       will yield prosperity for the people,
       and the hills righteousness.

4   May he judge with equity the poor of the people,
       saving the children of the needy
       and crushing the oppressor.

5   May the king worship you, the Lord,
       for as long as the sun and moon endure—
       ages without end.

6   Then he will be as showers on mown grass,
       as rain that waters the earth.

7   The righteous will flourish in abundant peace,
       as long as the moon continues to shine.

8   The king will rule from sea to sea,
       from the river to the ends of the earth.

9   Those living in the wilderness will pay him homage,
       his enemies will lick the dust.

10   The kings of Tarshish and the islands will pay tributes,
       and the kings of Sheba and Seba offer gifts.

11   Truly, all other kings will pay him homage—
       all nations serve under him.

12   For the king will come to the aid
       of the needy and the poor when they cry,

---

*Verses 18–20 are not part of the original psalm, but were added to mark the end of the Second Book of Psalms

	and all who have no-one to help them.
13	He will have pity on the weak and those in need, and save their lives.
14	He will redeem them from treachery and violence, for their lives are precious in his sight.
15	Long may he live! He will be given gold from Sheba. Prayers will be said continually for him, and he will be blessed each and every day.
16	Corn will grow even on the mountain-tops, the grains waving in abundance— the people will also flourish as copiously.
17	The king's renown will endure, his name known as long as the sun still shines. He will bless all people, and they in turn will call him blessed.
18	Blessed be the Lord, the God of Israel, who alone does amazing things.
19	May God's name be glorified forever and God's glory fill the whole earth. Amen and Amen
20	The prayers of David, son of Jesse, end here.

BOOK III

Psalms 73–89

Psalm 73

A teaching psalm which poses the question as to why the wicked flourish, concluding that, in the end, God will punish them

1   Truly, God is good to the people of Israel,
        especially those whose hearts are pure.

2   As for me, I had almost lost my footing
        and nearly fallen headlong.

3   For I let the prosperity of the wicked get to me—
        I envied the ease of the arrogant.

4–6   They do not struggle like the rest of us,
        are unconcerned with consequences,
        are sound of body, look top-class,
        dressed in the coat of injustice,
        the gold chains of pride.

7   They have much more than they need,
        but they want still more.

8   They speak as though they own the earth.
        They oppress others with impunity,
        and are corrupt to the core.

9   They speak ill even of heaven,
        and send fake messages over the earth.

10   They sit in the limelight,
     and seem to have it all,
     including the people's adulation.

11   Saying, "God does not care what we do.
     Does he even know?"

12   Look and see! It is those,
     who don't care a hoot about God,
     who keep on getting wealthier,
     and prosper in this world of ours.

13   And look at me.
     In vain did I keep myself pure.
     ritually and spiritually.

14   Where has it got me?
     Every morning I feel guilty,
     and suffer doubts all day long.

15   If I talk about this,
     people take offense.

16   It is just too much to understand
     how it all works.

17   Then I went into God's sanctuary,
     and it all became clear—

18   God does indeed set the wicked
     on a slippery slope,
     making them fall to their ruin.

19   Their end will come in an instant,
     when they will be swept away in terror.

20   In your mind, O God, they will vanish
     as a dream does on waking.

21   When I was upset by all of this,
     sore at heart,

22   I was being a fool,
     ignorant and beastly.

Psalm 74

23	Yet you held me by my right hand,
	and did not banish me from your presence.
24	You guided me with your counsel,
	and will one day receive me in glory.
25	Whom have I in heaven but you?
	and on earth you are all I desire.
26	For even though my flesh and my mind may fail me,
	you, God, are my strength,
	and more than enough for me forever.
27	For indeed, those far from you will perish.
	You will destroy those who are unfaithful to you.
28	How good it is for me
	to draw near to you, O God,
	to put my trust in you,
	and to tell of all you have done.

Psalm 74

A national prayer for help on being invaded, probably written during the Babylonian invasion in 586 BCE

1	O God, why have you abandoned us?
	Will it be forever?
	Why are you fuming with anger
	at your own sheep?
2	Remember your people,
	your inheritance which you redeemed,
	this mount of Zion where you lived.
3	Do something about the desolation the enemy has wrought,
	wickedly destroying your sanctuary.
4	In the very center where your people met
	they have set up their own banners as symbols.

PSALM 74

5   Once a man became famous by cutting down trees
and carving the wood.

6   Now they use axes and hammers to destroy
the carver's work in seconds.

7   They have defiled the place where your name resided
by pulling it to the ground and setting it on fire.

8   In their hearts they planned to destroy everything together,
so they set fire to every meeting-place in the land.

9   They have destroyed all our distinguishing symbols
and there is no longer a prophet in the land—
no-one to tell us how long.

10   How long is the adversary going to mock?
Is the enemy going to blaspheme your name forever?

11   While you sit with your hands in your lap,
and do not lift a finger to help us.

12   For God, you are our king of old,
you are the one whose actions saved us

13   When you divided the sea by your power,
and smashed the heads of the dragons in the waters.

14   You cut up the sea-monster, Leviathan, as meat
for the creatures of the desert.

15   You split rocks for fountains to gush out.
You dried up mighty rivers.

16   The day is yours, the night as well—
you set the moon and the sun.

17   You fixed the earth's dimensions.
You created summer and winter.

18   Remember O Lord, how the enemy reviles you,
how nonbelievers insult your name.

19   Do not deliver the life of your dove to wild animals,
and do not forget the plight of the afflicted forever.

21   Honor your covenant,
for the dark places of the earth
are haunted by cruelty and violence.

Psalm 75

| 21 | Do not leave the oppressed in shame. |
| | Rather may the poor and needy praise you. |

22	Those who do not believe in you
	use our name as a swear-word.
	Do not ignore this, but stand up to them,

| 23 | For the shouts of the enemy |
| | are growing ever more vociferous against you. |

Psalm 75*

Praise to God who judges rightly—one of the oldest of the psalms

1	We give you our thanks, O God,
	we give you our thanks,
	as we tell of what you have done for us.

| 2 | "When all the people appear before me, |
| | I will judge rightly." you declare. |

| 3 | "When the earth shakes and its inhabitants totter, |
| | I will hold it steady. |

| 4 | To the arrogant I say, stop boasting, |
| | and to the violent, do not flex your muscles. |

| 5 | Do not blow your own trumpet, |
| | and do not test your strength against mine. |

| 6 | You will not be promoted |
| | from any of the four corners of the globe." |

| 7 | For God alone is the judge— |
| | with power to put one down and lift another up high. |

| 8 | In God's hand is a cup of foaming wine. |

---

* In the Hebrew it is clear that this psalm uses the *horn* as a motif. (See Glossary for *horn*) This is lost in translation. It occurs in:
vs 4: *do not lift your horn…*
vs 5: *do not raise your horn…*
vs 10: *all the horns of the wicked…*

　　　　Once the impurities settle on the bottom,
　　　　God pours off the good wine
　　　　and all the wicked of the earth will
　　　　drink the dregs—to the very last drop.

10　　　God will cut off all the boasts and powers
　　　　of the wicked,
　　　　but the powers of the righteous
　　　　will continue to grow.

9　　　As for me I will forever sing
　　　　praises to my God,
　　　　the God of Jacob and Rachel.

Psalm 76

A song of national thanksgiving—God is to be feared

1　　　In Judah God is known,
　　　　in Israel his name is great.

2　　　In Salem he has his sanctuary,
　　　　in Zion his dwelling place.

3　　　There God destroyed all the weapons of war—
　　　　which put an end to the battle itself.

4　　　God, you are more glorious, more majestic
　　　　than the enduring mountains.

5　　　The bravest in the army are defeated—
　　　　they are knocked unconscious,
　　　　so that none can brandish a weapon.

6　　　At your mighty command, O God of Jacob,
　　　　both rider and horse lie stunned.

7　　　Indeed, you are to be feared.
　　　　When you are angry who can stand before you?

| 8 | When you pronounce judgement from heaven, |
| | all the earth stops in fear. |

| 9 | You arrive to judge us all, |
| | and to save the oppressed. |

10	Even the anger of us humans
	will be turned into praise of you.
	You will prevent it from doing harm.

11	Make your vows to the Lord
	and carry them out.
	Everyone, bring gifts to him.

12	Our God is the one to be revered,
	far above the kings and princes of this world,
	for they are all in his thrall.

Psalm 77

Crying to God in distress

1	I cried out to God—
	I cried aloud to God,
	so that he could hear me.

2	During the day I brought my distress to God.
	At night it ran on without ceasing.
	My soul could find no comfort.

3	I remembered God but was still upset.
	I complained—
	my spirit down in the depths.

| 4 | My eyes would not close in sleep— |
| | my suffering too great to put into words, |

| 5 | Memories came of the past— |
| | of days long gone. |

6	I recalled songs I used to sing, I meditated, I searched my spirit, and voiced my doubts.
7	Will the Lord reject me forever? Will he never favor me again?
8	Has his mercy deserted me for good? Will his promises mean nothing from now on?
9	Has God forgotten to be gracious? Has his anger cut off his tender love?
10	I wondered if God himself was sick – if his right-hand had withered to prevent him from acting.
11	I will call to mind your works, O Lord. I will always remember your wonders of old.
12	I will number all your actions, and tell others what you have done.
13	Your way is holy. Is there any God as great as ours?
14	You are the wonder-working God. You have shown your strength to the people.
15	With your strong arms you redeemed your people, the descendants of Jacob and Rachel.
16	The waters saw you, O God and they were afraid. The waters saw you and they trembled into their depths.
17	The clouds poured out water. The skies thundered. The lightning was like shot arrows.
18	The skies reverberated with thunder. Your lightning bolts lit up the earth. The whole world trembled and shook.

19	Your way is through the sea,
	your path through the oceans,
	so that no-one sees your footsteps.
20	Lead your people like a flock—
	with Moses and Aaron leading the way.

Psalm 78

A teaching psalm, recounting the history of the Israelites from the Exodus to David's reign.

1	Listen, my people, to my teaching,
	incline your ears to the words of my mouth.
2	I will teach in parables,
	using deep sayings of old,
3	Reiterating what we have all heard and know,
	because our fathers and mothers imparted them to us.
4	We will not hide them from our children,
	but tell them to the generations to come—
	the splendor of the Lord, his victories,
	and the wonderful things he has done.
5	God established a rule of life in Jacob's land,
	and appointed a law in Israel,
	which he commanded that our ancestors
	teach to their children,
6	That the next generation should know them,
	the children not yet born,
	and that they in turn should tell their children,
7	So that they, each one, put their hope in God,
	never forget his deeds,
	and keep his commandments.

Psalm 78

8   May they not be like their ancestors,
stubborn and rebellious—
their hearts not set in the right direction,
their spirit not dedicated to God.

9   Call to mind the Ephraimites,
who, though armed,
turned back on the day of battle.

10   They did not honor God's covenant,
and refused to live by his law.

11   They forgot what he had done—
ignored the miracles he had done for them.

12   In the sight of their ancestors
he had done wondrous things,
in the land of Egypt,
in the fields of Zoan.

13   He split the sea in two,
and enabled them to walk through,
while the water stood like a cliff.

14   He led them during the day with a cloud,
and at night with the light of a fire.

15   He split rocks in the wilderness,
which gave them water to drink from the depths.

16   So abundant was the water,
it streamed out to form rivers.

17   Yet they went on sinning against the God above all others,
rebelling against him in the desert.

18   They tested his patience by demanding the food they craved,
even taunting him by asking,
"Can God set a feast in the wilderness?"

19   And this was after he struck the rock,
so that the water gushed out.

20	Then they asked. "Can God give his people bread? And what about meat? Can he provide that?"
21	When God heard this he was filled with rage— his anger blazed against Jacob and Israel,
22	Because they had no faith in their God, and still would not trust in his power to save.
23-25	Even so, he opened the doors of heaven, and commanded the clouds above to rain down manna for them to eat, giving them the grain of heaven, the food of angels for the people of earth. They ate their fill.
26	Then he caused the wind to blow from the east, and by his power a wind from the south.
27	With this, like a dust storm bringing all the sand of the desert, feathered birds rained down on them.
28, 29	God even made them fall within their camp, just where they had pitched their tents. They ate their fill. God gave them what they craved.
30	But while they were still eating, they carried straight on complaining.
31	So God finally lost his temper with them, and killed the strongest among them, the pride of their people.
32	Despite these miracles, they still did not trust in God, but they went on sinning.
33	Therefore God caused their days to pass without progress and their years in trouble.
34	Only when some among them died, did they stop and think of God, and turn again to him.
35	Only then did they remember

Psalm 78

that God was the rock,
and the High God their redeemer.

36 But their flattery of God only went as far as their mouths.
Their tongues lied to him,

37 For their hearts were not right with him.
They were not true to his covenant.

38 But God, full of compassion,
forgave their sins,
and did not destroy them.
Many a time he had to keep his anger in check,
and put a lid on his wrath.

39 He kept in mind that they were but mortals,
a breeze blowing past never to return.

40 They provoked him often enough in the wilderness,
and caused him grief enough in the desert.

41 They tempted him to lose his temper,
and limited what the Holy One of Israel could do,

42 Because they ignored his hand held out to help
and forgot the way he delivered them
from their oppressors—

43 How he had done this with miracles in Egypt
and wonders in the plain of Zoan.

44 God turned their rivers into blood,
so that their enemy could not drink the water.

45 He sent plagues of flies to torment them
and frogs to destroy them.

46 God sent caterpillars to devour their grain,
and locusts to destroy their crops.

47 Their vines he destroyed with hail,
and their fig trees with frost.

48 Hail and lightning killed their cattle.

49 But the fiercest of his anger, and indignation,
God vented on them by setting loose destroying angels.

Psalm 78

50   He went as far as taking their very lives,
    sending a plague among them.

51   God killed all the first-born in Egypt,
    the symbols of their power, in the tents of Ham.

52   He brought his own people out,
    and led them like a flock of sheep through the wilderness.

53   God led them on safely, so that they had no fears,
    while their oppressors were overwhelmed by the sea.

54   He brought them to his holy mount,
    to the place his right hand had bought.

55   God cast out the heathen who were there,
    gave their dwellings to the tribes of Israel,
    divided between them as their inheritance.

56   Yet they kept on provoking and testing the God above all others,
    and did not observe his decrees.

57   They became renegades and as faithless as their ancestors,
    as useless as a slack bow.

58   They angered him with their pagan places of worship,
    and made him jealous with their idols.

59   When God heard of this,
    it made him extremely angry
    and he was done with Israel.

60   He abandoned his dwelling in Shiloh,
    the tent where he lived among mortals,

61   Delivered his fortress to the captives,
    and his glorious ark into the oppressor's hands.

62   God gave his people to the sword,
    so enraged was he with them.

63   The fire devoured their young men
    and there was no-one to marry their young women.

64   Their priests fell by the sword,
    and their widows could make no sound of lamentation.

65 At this the Lord awoke as from a deep sleep,
and like a great man shouting from too much wine,

66 He routed the enemy from the rear.
and put them permanently out of action.

67 This was when God rejected Joseph's people
and did not choose the tribe of Ephraim.

68 But chose the tribe of Judah
and Mount Zion which he loved.

69 God built his place of worship at the
meeting place of high heaven and the earth
which he had created from before time.

70 He chose David to be his servant
and fetched him from the sheepfold.

71 From looking after sheep he brought him
to shepherd the people of Jacob and Israel,
God's heritage.

72 David shepherded them with integrity of heart,
and guided them with skillful hands.

Psalm 79

A cry of anguish after Jerusalem is destroyed

1 O God, the nations who do not worship you
have invaded your inheritance.
They have defiled your holy temple.
They have reduced Jerusalem to a heap of rubble.

2 The corpses of your servants
have become food for the birds of the air,
the flesh of those who believe in you,
meat for the animals of the earth.

3 Their blood has flown like water in and around Jerusalem.
No-one has been spared to bury them.

Psalm 79

4   We have become a joke to our neighbors,
        and held in derision by those around us.

5   For how long, O Lord?
        Will you be angry from now on?
        Will your jealousy burn on like fire?

6   Rather pour your wrath upon those who do not believe in you,
        and upon those nations who do not call on your name.

7   For they have devoured Jacob,
        and laid waste all his dwellings.

8   Do not lay at our door iniquities of old.
        Let your tender mercies rather come to meet us,
        for we are now down and out.

9   Help us, O God of our salvation,
        for the glory of your name.
        Deliver us, and wash away our sins,
        for the sake of your reputation.

10   Why should the nations ask, "Where is their God?"
        Let us see your name become known
        as the God who avenges the blood of his servants.

11   Let the groans of those taken captive come before you,
        for your power is great enough to help them.

12   Pay back seven-fold to our neighbors,
        right into their very souls, the taunts
        with which they have taunted you, O Lord,

13   So that we, your people, and the sheep of your fold,
        may give you thanks for ever.
        We will praise you generation after generation
        for all to see.

Psalm 80

*A plea for help for the nation, which is likened to a vine.
If God returns to them, they will be saved*

1, 2   Give us your ear, O Shepherd of Israel—
lead Joseph like a flock.
Shine out in front of Ephraim, Benjamin and Manasseh.
You, whose throne is between the cherubim,
in your full strength come and save us.

3   *O God, return to us,
smile on us,
and we shall be saved.*

4   O Lord God Almighty,
how long will you be angry while your people pray?

5   You are feeding us with the bread of tears.
and to drink we have bottles full of tears.

6   You are making us a joke among our neighbors,
and a laughing point among our enemies.

7   *O God, return to us,
smile on us,
and we shall be saved.*

8   You brought a vine out of Egypt,
and after driving out those who did not believe in you,
you planted it.

9   You prepared the ground for it,
so that it took deep root,
and grew to fill the land.

10   Its shadow covered the hills,
and its branches grew like the stately cedars.

11   They even touched the sea on the one side
and the river on the other.

12   Why have you now broken down its hedges
so that anyone passing by can pick its fruit?

13	Even the boars come from the woods to feast on it and the wild animals from the fields devour it.
14	O God Almighty, return to us, we implore you. Look down from heaven and see us. Come and visit your vine again.
15	Take care of the vineyard you planted with your own hands. Take care of the person you strengthened for yourself.
16	For it has been cut down and burned in the fire. May those who did this perish as you turn to face them with your rebuke.
17	But let your hand be on the one on your right, on the person you made strong for yourself.
18	Then we will never forsake you. Bring us back to life again, and we will walk with you.
19	*O Lord God Almighty, return to us! smile on us, and we shall be saved.*

Psalm 81

The first part - a festival hymn of North Israel. The second part— God speaks, reminding the people how he led them from Egypt.

1	Sing aloud to God our strength— sing with joy to the God of Jacob and of Rachel.
2	Sing a song and beat the drum. Sing in harmony with lyre and harp.

Psalm 81

3	Blow the trumpet on our appointed day— at the new moon, our feast day,
4, 5	For this was ordained for Israel, a statute of the God of Jacob, a law of Joseph's God as a testimony to the time when he came to us in the land of Egypt. There he spoke to us in a language that we did not know.
6	So God reminds us, "I relieved your shoulders from their burdens, your hands from lifting the baskets.
7	When you cried out in trouble, I freed you. I heard you from my secret place of thunder, though you tested me at the waters of Meribah.
8	O my people, if you would only listen to what I tell you— pay attention to my words.
9	Let there be no other strange god among you— let there be no other god that you worship.
10	I am the Lord your God. I was the one who brought you out of captivity in Egypt, and filled your wide-open mouths.
11	But would my people listen to my voice? No, this people of Israel would have none of me.
12	So I left them to lust to their heart's desire, and to walk in their own way.
13	O, I wish they had listened to me and walked in my way!
14	I would have quickly subdued their enemies, and worked against those who are against them.
15	Then those who hated me, the Lord, would cringe before me, their doom sealed forever.

16   O my people, I wanted to feed you with the finest wheat,
and with honey out of the rock to your fill."

Psalm 82

*As Chief Justice God rules against the lesser gods
and their unjust rule—a very ancient psalm*

1   Judgement begins in the High Court of the gods,
where God takes his place as the Chief Justice.

2   He pronounces judgement:
"How long will you give unjust judgements
in favor of the wicked?

3   Defend the weak and the orphan,
and show the poor and needy true justice.

4   Set them free
from the clutches of the wicked.

5   They are in the dark
because they do not know
or understand the way things work,
and now the whole world is out of balance.

6   As for all of you, I had thought,
as children of the god above all,
you too were gods,

7   Yet you will die like any ordinary person,
and fall as even royalty falls."

8   Rise up, O God, be the judge of all on earth,
for all nations belong to you.

Psalm 83

A national lament against the alliance of surrounding nations in a conspiracy to defeat them

1. O God, do not stay silent!
   Do not hold your peace!
   Do not sit still!

2. For look, your enemies are beginning to cause a stir.
   Those who hate you are lifting their heads to strike.

3. They are cleverly plotting against your people,
   and conspiring against those under your protection.

4. Their plan: "We will obliterate them as a nation,
   so that the name of Israel will be forgotten."

5. These are co-operating with one goal –
   these who have allied themselves against you:

6. The Ishmaelites and the inhabitants of Edom,
   of Moab and the Hagarites,

7. Gebal, Ammon and Amalek,
   together with the Philistines,
   and the people of Tyre.

8. Assyria has also joined them,
   as the strong arm of the children of Lot.

9. Do to them as you did to Midian,
   as you did to Sisera
   and to Jabin at the Wadi Kishon.

10. You destroyed them at Endor,
    so totally that they became manure for the soil.

11. Make the fate of their nobles like that of Oreb and Zeeb,
    and the princes of Zebah and Zalmunna,

12. Whose intention was to possess the pastures of God.

13. O my God, make them whirl around like tumbleweed,
    blow away like stubble before the wind.

14	May they be like a forest set alight, a mountain burning before a wildfire.
15	Let them feel the power of one of your tempests, the full brunt of one of your storms.
16	May they be so filled with shame that they will beg you for mercy.
17	May they be forever in turmoil and in terror – may they be fully disgraced and then vanish.
18	Then all of humanity will know that you, whose name is The Lord, are the God above all gods on the earth.

Psalm 84

Happy are those who worship and live in God's house

1	How lovely is the place where you live, O Lord God Almighty.
2	My soul longs, even faints with longing, to be with you in your house. With my whole body and all my desire I cry out for your living presence, O God.
3	The sparrow has even found a home, and the swallow built a nest, where she will tend her young, right near your altar, O Lord, my King and my God.
4	Those that live in your house are happy indeed, constantly filled with praise for you.
5	Happy are those whose strength is in you, as they journey on the road to Zion.
6	As they pass through the valley of Baca,

instead of misery,
may they find a place filled with springs and pools
from the early rains.

7 May they go from strength to strength
as they look forward to meeting
their God in Zion.

8 Hear my prayer,
O Lord God Almighty,
listen to me, O God of Jacob and Rachel.

9 Look and see,
O God, our shield,
Look with favor
on the face of your anointed one.

10 For a day in your house is better
than a thousand elsewhere.
I would rather stand on the threshold
of the house of my God than live
in the houses of wickedness.

11 For you, Lord, my God,
are sun and shield to me.
You will give me grace and honor,
for you withhold nothing good
from those who walk in the way of integrity.

12 O Lord God Almighty,
How happy are those
who put their trust in you.

Psalm 85

Appeal for rain in a drought or for renewal of faith in a "dry" period, so that love and integrity may kiss

1. Lord, show favor to your land!
   Restore the fortunes of Jacob!

2. Forgive the wrongdoing of your people.
   Pardon all their sin.

3. Put aside your wrath.
   Turn away from your anger.

4. Come back to us, O God of our well-being,
   and stop being so annoyed with us,

5. Or are you going to be angry with us from now on?
   Will your anger pass from this generation to the next?

6. Will you not renew us,
   so that everyone finds their joy in you?

7. Show your mercy to us, O Lord,
   and enable us to flourish.

8. I hear what the Lord our God has to say—
   he indeed talks of well-being for his people,
   for his faithful people,
   but they must not return to foolishness.

9. In truth, his bounty is close
   to those who are devoted to him,
   and this will make our land flourish.

10. Unfailing love and integrity will kiss.
    Righteousness and peace will embrace.

11. Compassion will sprout from the earth,
    and justice will rain down from the skies.

12. Indeed, Lord God, you will give us
    exactly the rain we need,
    and the land will produce in abundance.

13   Righteousness will go before you,
     and you will make a path,
     so that we can follow in your steps.

Psalm 86

*An individual pleads for help, forgiveness,
and victory over his enemies*

1   Bend your ear, O Lord, to my prayer,
    for I am poor and in need.

2   I trust in you, my God,
    I am devoted to you.
    Guard your servant
    and save my life.

3   Have pity on me,
    for I call to you all day long.

4   Let your servant be joyful in spirit,
    for I present to you all that I am.

5   You, O Lord, are goodness itself,
    ready to forgive and to accept
    all those who call out to you.

6   Bend your ear, O Lord, to my prayer.
    Listen to my appeal.

7   In the day when trouble comes my way
    I call out to you,
    for I know you will answer me.

8   You are unique among all the gods
    that people worship.
    None of them can accomplish what you do.

Psalm 86

9   All the nations you created
shall come and worship you, O God,
and give glory to your name.

10   For you are great—
you do amazing things—
the only God who does.

11   Teach me your way, O Lord.
I would walk in your truth.
May each part of me be united
in worship of your name.

12   I want to praise you, O Lord, my God,
from deep within my heart.
I desire to give glory to your name
from now and forever.

13   For you have generously
shown me your mercy,
delivering my soul from
the depths of hell.

14   O God, the insolent—
those who reject you,
have now turned against me.
A gang of thugs is after my life.

15   You, O God, on the other hand,
are full of compassion, mercy and grace,
and overflowing with patience and goodness.

16   O look on me, your servant, with pity.
Give me strength enough to save me.
Give me, your faithful child, victory.

17   Work a miracle for me that can be seen
by those who hate me,
so that they will be ashamed of their actions.
For it is you, O Lord, who can help me
and give me support.

Psalm 87

In praise of Zion, city of God

1. The city God founded stands on the holy mountain.
2. God loves even the gates of this city
   more than all the dwellings of Jacob's descendants.
3. Glorious things are told of you, Zion, city of our God,
4. To those who know me, I may mention
   Egypt and Babylon,
   or maybe say that so and so was born in
   Tyre, in Philistia, or in Ethiopia,
5. But of Zion it is said,
   "He or she was born in her
   whom the Lord alone established".
6. And the Lord, when writing it
   in the book of records, will write.
   "This one was born there."
7. Singers and dancers alike say,
   "All my inspiration springs from you."

Psalm 88

A cry of desolation from one who has suffered long

1. O Lord, God of my salvation.
   I call out to you night and day.
2. Bend your ear to my cry!
   Turn, and listen to my prayer.
3. For life for me is just trouble,
   as even now it draws to a close.

Psalm 88

4 I am like one who is at death's door—
   one with no strength at all.

5 Or among those already dead—
   those already slain and in Sheol,
   cut off from your helping hand
   because they are already forgotten.

6 You have laid me out in the lowest grave,
   way down in the depths
   where there is only darkness.

7 Your anger is pressed heavily on me.
   It comes at me in overwhelming waves.

8 You have made me so repulsive to my friends,
   that they have all left me.
   I am shut off from everyone,
   and there is no escape.

9 My eyes grow dim with anguish,
   as every day I call on you for help,
   pleading with outspread hands.

10 Can the dead rise up
   and see your wonderful deeds?
   Can they get up and praise you?

11 Is your tender love available in the grave?
   Your faithfulness once life has already gone?

12 Are your wonders known in the darkest place?
   Your goodness in the land of forgetfulness?

13 Meanwhile all the time I still cry out to you, O Lord—
   every morning I appeal to you again.

14 O Lord, why have you rejected me?
   Why have you turned your back on me?

15 I have suffered and been near death from an early age,
   and now I feel numb from the pain.

16 Your fierce rages roar over me,
   your onslaughts overwhelm me,

17   As they wash over me in waves every day,
hemming me in.

18   You have cut me off
from all my friends and neighbors.
My only companion now—
utter darkness.

Psalm 89

*A royal psalm—praise and entreaty by the king
for deliverance from his enemies*

1   I will forever sing
of your loving kindness, O Lord.
I will proclaim your faithfulness
to all generations.

2   I will say how you have been building up
mercy upon mercy forever,
and how your faithfulness
was first established in heaven.

3   And how you promised:
"I have made a covenant with my chosen one,
with David, my servant,
I have sworn this.

4   Your descendants
will be here forever,
and your throne for all generations".

5   In the heavens they praise
this promise, O Lord,
and in the congregation
your faithfulness.

6   Who in heaven can be compared
to our Lord?

Psalm 89

     Who among the heavenly beings
     can come close to our God?

7   You are held in the greatest reverence
     by the faithful congregation,
     in total awe by those
     who gather around you.

8   O Lord God Almighty,
     who is as strong a god as you?
     Who has faithfulness
     that can be compared to yours?

9   You are the one who rules
     the waves of the sea—
     when they rise too high,
     you calm them.

10   You have scattered your enemies
     with your strong arm,
     slaying and scattering in pieces
     the monster Rahab.

11   Both heaven and earth belong to you,
     the world and everything in it,
     for you made it all.

12   From the North to the South—
     you created it all.
     Both Tabor and Herman
     rejoice in your presence.

13   Yours is a strong rule.
     You rule with a mighty hand,
     a hand raised high.

14   Justice and rights are alive in your rule—
     love and truth stand before you.

15   The people who know this are happy,
     as they walk under your beaming smile.

16   They rejoice all day together—
     they are jubilant over your generosity.

17 Your favor increases their strength,
    exalts it and brings it renown.

18 For the Lord is our refuge,
    and the holy one of Israel is our sovereign.

19 Once you spoke in a vision
    to one holy in your sight
    and said: "I chose a young man instead of a warrior,
    an unknown instead of a hero.

20 I found David, my servant,
    and anointed him with holy oil.

21 My ruling hand will be behind him,
    and my arm will give him strength.

22 The enemy will not outwit him,
    nor the worst of evildoers overpower him.

23 For I will cut down his foes in front of him,
    and defeat those who hate him.

24 My faithfulness and mercy will go with him,
    and he will go from strength to strength.

25 His one hand will be over the sea,
    his other over the river.

26 He will call out to me,
    'You are my Father, my God,
    and the solid foundation of my safekeeping.'

27 I will make him my first-born,
    and he will be higher than all the kings on earth.

28 I will be merciful to him forever,
    and my covenant will stand unbroken between us.

29 His descendants will last forever,
    and his rule as long as the heavens endure.

30 But if his offspring abandon my law,
    and do not follow my rule,

31 If they break my commands,
    and do not keep to my way of life,

Psalm 89

32	Then I will come at their sins with a rod, and their iniquities will draw stripes from me.
33	Even so, I will not withdraw my compassion from them completely, nor will I be unfaithful to them.
34	I will not break my side of the covenant, nor go back on my word.
35	What I swore to David will never become null and void,
36, 37	For his offspring will endure forever and his throne last as long as the sun and the moon continue to shine— and they are faithful witnesses in the skies."
38, 39	Yet now we feel it is you who have cancelled the covenant— you have been angry with your anointed, and thrown him out in revulsion. You denounced his crown and threw it on the ground.
40	And you have broken down the walls around his strongholds, bringing them to ruin.
41	Now all passers-by help themselves to what was his. His neighbors mock him.
42	You have strengthened the hand of his antagonists, giving his enemies cause to rejoice.
43	You blunted his sword so that he had no leg to stand on in the battle.
44	You have cut short his fame, and upended his throne.
45	You have bedecked him with shame, and his youth has fled before its time.
46	How long, O Lord, will this go on? How long will you rage like a burning fire?
47	You have allotted to each one such a short time. So, is all in vain?

48	Where is the one who will not see death? Where is the one who will escape from Sheol?
49	Lord, you truly swore to be forever compassionate to your servant David. What has happened to that now?
50	Keep in mind, O God, the disgrace your servant bears, how the taunting of nonbelievers has pierced him deep in his heart.
51	While your enemies also throw insults, and harass the footsteps of your anointed one.
52*	May the Lord be blessed forever. Amen and Amen.

---

* This verse has been added to mark the end of the third of the five books of psalms.

BOOK IV

Psalms 90–106

Psalm 90

*A lament on the brevity, only "two score years and ten",
and misery, of life*

1   Lord, you have been our refuge
       through each and every generation.

2   And you have been our God forever and ever,
       from before the mountains were formed,
       before the earth was in existence,
       even before you made the universe.

3   When you say, "Return to dust, human beings,"
       we become dust again.

4   For a thousand years in your sight
       are like yesterday gone—
       like a watch in the night.

5, 6   You carry us away as in a flood,
       or as in a dream on waking,
       or like grass growing—
       in the morning it springs up and flourishes,
       by evening it is withered and mowed down.

8   For you have laid bare
       our wrongdoing before you,
       seen our secret sins
       in the light of your vision,

7	And turned your wrath on us to unsettle us and end our days.
9	For all our days are lived under your anger, Our years slip away like a sigh.
10	The years allotted to us are just seventy. We may reach eighty, but it will be in toil and trouble. They fly past in no time, and we are gone.
11	Who knows the extent of your anger? As much as we fear you, so much is your anger.
12	So teach us to value each day, that we may gain a heart of wisdom.
13	Turn your anger away from us, O Lord, Turn around and change your perspective.
14	Pour enough mercy on us to satisfy our longing to be full of joy and gladness all our days.
15	Match our troubles year for year with gladness, all the evil we have seen year for year with joy.
16	Let your servants see you at work, and let their children behold your glory.
17	Pour your beauty, O Lord our God, on us and bring to fulfilment the work of our hands— Yes, Lord! Bring to fulfilment the work of our hands.

Psalm 91

Assurance of God's protection, especially against disease and accident

1. Those who live under the protection
   of the God who is greatest,
   who rest in the shadow of God Almighty,

2. Say of the Lord: "He is my God,
   a refuge and fortress to me.
   In God I trust."

3. God will rescue you from the snare that entangles you,
   and from any threatening plague.

4. You will rest secure under his wings,
   and he will cover you with his feathers.
   His truth will be your shield and buckler.

5. You will not be afraid of any night-time terrors,
   nor of any day-time scourges.

6. Nor of any attacks in the dark,
   nor any malaise in broad daylight.

7. Even though thousands are succumbing,
   on your right and on your left,
   you will not be overcome.

8. You will also see with your own eyes
   what fate awaits the wicked.

9. If you have made the Lord your refuge,
   the God above all others your abode,

10. No evil will attack you,
    no plague will get even close to your house.

11. For God will put you in the care of his angels.
    They will keep you safe in all you do.

12. If you are about to stub your foot on a stone,
    they will be there to keep you from falling.

13	You will tread on any lion or adder that threatens you,
	and trample underfoot their young.
14	God gives us this assurance,
	"Because you have loved me,
	I will deliver you.
	Because you have valued my name,
	I will hold yours up high.
15	When you call on me, I will answer,
	when you are in trouble, I will be with you.
	I will give you freedom with honor.
16	You will have salvation and a long satisfying life".

Psalm 92

The song of an individual thanking God for the gift of joy, strength and flourishing

1	It is good to give you thanks, O God,
	good to sing praises in your honor, O God above all.
2	Good to sing of your compassion every morning,
	and your faithfulness each night,
3	Accompanied by stringed instruments,
	by a lyre and a harp.
4	For you have made me rejoice, O Lord, in your actions.
	Your deeds have given me joy.
5	Yes, Lord, your deeds are great indeed,
	and your mind immense.
6	Unfathomable by anyone,
	let alone the unthinking and foolish.
7	If the wicked flourish
	and the crooked spring up like weeds,
	they do so to their own destruction.

Psalm 93

8   You, O Lord, are the God above all others forever.

9   And surely all your enemies, all the evildoers,
       will be no more—they will all be blown away.

10   You will increase my strength.
       It will be legendary, like that of a wild ox.
       I will be anointed with fresh oil.

11   My eye will see what I long to see—
       the end of my enemy.
       My ear will hear what I long to hear—
       my attackers are no more.

12   The just will flourish like a palm tree—
       they will grow tall like a cedar in Lebanon.

13   Those who are planted in your house
       will thrive in your courts.

14   They will bear fruit even in old age.
       They will flourish and keep on growing.

15   This will show how perfectly good you are, O Lord.
       There is not even a hint of wrong in you.
       You, O God, are my rock.

Psalm 93

The Lord has reigned forever—from before time began

1   The Lord reigns,
       clothed in majesty,
       encircled with strength,
       for it was the Lord who established the world,
       and set it in its place.

2   And, Lord, your throne existed
       even before that—

    from before time began.

3   The sea may come crashing in, wave after wave,
    in thundering, pounding breakers,
    making their roaring voices heard,

4   But you are mightier than them,
    than wave after mighty wave in the sea—
    mightier than high heaven itself.

5   The evidence is very sure—
    your whole house is holy, O Lord,
    day in, day out, forever.

Psalm 94

*The God of vengeance takes care of the righteous,
and will destroy the wicked*

1   O Lord God, vengeance is yours—
    it belongs to you, O God.
    Show yourself to us.

2   Act now, O judge of the earth,
    and exact payment from the arrogant.

3   Lord, how long,
    O how long are the wicked
    going to be the victors?

4   How long are they going to rule harshly,
    and then boast of their deeds?

5   They are inflicting wounds on your inheritance,
    and crushing your people.

6   They destroy the widow and the foreigner,
    and kill the orphan,

Psalm 94

7   All the while claiming,
    "The Lord will not see.
    The God of Jacob
    will take no notice."

8   Understand this, you fools.
    Wake up to reality, you dullards.

9   The one who formed the ear,
    is he deaf?
    The one who fashioned the eye,
    is he blind?

10 The one who puts the nonbelievers right,
    will he not correct his own?
    The one who first taught us to know,
    does he know nothing?

11 You do indeed know every one of our thoughts,
    and you know how futile they are.

12 For blessed is the one you correct, O Lord,
    and the one who learns your law.

13 May you give him respite from the days of trouble,
    until the wicked are dead and buried.

14 For you, Lord will not reject your people,
    nor will you abandon your estate.

15 With judgement will come justice,
    and all those whose ways are right
    will follow that way.

16 The question God asks is:
    "Who will rouse themselves for me
    against the wrongdoers?
    Who will stand up for me
    against the actively evil?"

17 Unless the Lord had been there helping me,
    my life would have been worth nothing.

18 When I cried out that my foot was slipping,

	you held me up, O Lord of mercy.
19	When my thoughts were all in a muddle, your comfort made me happy again.
20	Can the circles of evil have fellowship with you? The inventor of evil, receive your protection?
21	They band together to destroy the very center of righteousness, and to condemn the innocent.
22	But the Lord is the rock who keeps me safe— always there to defend me.
23	The Lord our God will wipe them out, by making their own evil turn on the wicked, and their own malice their downfall.

Psalm 95

A call to thanksgiving and a warning not to harden your hearts and forget God

1.	O come! Come, and sing to our Lord! Make a joyful noise before the Rock who saves us.
2	Come into his presence with thanksgiving, singing loud songs of praise.
3	For the Lord is a great God, and a great King, above all other gods.
4	He made all that exists, and holds it in his hands, from the depths of the earth to the mountain heights,
5	From the wide oceans to the dry land— he made it all.

PSALM 96

6   So come before him to worship.
        Bow down before God our creator.

7   We are his people, the sheep in his flock,
        and he is our God.
        Listen to what he says today—

8, 9   "Do not harden your hearts
        as your ancestors did at Meribah
        and at Massah in the wilderness,
        on the day they provoked me
        and put me to the test,
        though they had seen what I could do.

10   For forty long years I was against them.
        They had gone astray in their hearts,
        because they rejected my ways.

11   In my anger I swore
        that they would not enter
        the place of rest."

PSALM 96

*Rejoice because the Lord is great,
and is coming to govern the whole world*

1   O sing to the Lord a new song.
        Come sing to the Lord, all the earth.

2   Sing to the Lord! Bless his name,
        and tell of his salvation all day long.

3   Proclaim his glory among the nations,
        his wonder among all peoples.

4   Give him great praise, for he is great!
        Praise him in awe, for he is awesome!
        He is above all the other gods.

5   They are idols, made by human hands,
        but the Lord himself made the heavens.

6   Before him go honor and majesty—
        at his side beauty and strength.

7   Come with your families and
        give to the Lord glory and strength.

8   Give to the Lord the glory his name deserves.
        Bring an offering to the Lord in his sanctuary,

9   And worship him in the beauty of holiness.
        Be awe-struck before him, all on earth.

10   Tell all nonbelievers that the Lord is in charge.
        He has set an order that will not be shaken,
        and he will be the judge of who is just.

11   Let the heavens rejoice
        and the earth be glad,
        Let the sea roar in all its fulness.

12   Let the fields be joyful and all in them.
        May even the trees in the woodlands rejoice
        before the Lord.

13   The Lord is coming!
        He is coming to govern the whole world.
        He will govern all people on earth
        with justice and in truth.

Psalm 97

Praise-song to God who reigns in justice

1   The Lord reigns! Let the earth rejoice!
        From isle to isle, let all exult!

2   He is surrounded by clouds and darkness,
        but righteousness and justice live on his throne.

3   Fire precedes him
    and blazes behind him.

4   He lights the whole world with lightning,
    and those who see it tremble.

5   The mountains melt like wax at the Lord's presence—
    the presence of the Lord of the whole world.

6   The heavens above declare his righteousness,
    and all the people below see his glory.

7   May those who worship hand-made images,
    those who boast of their own gods,
    be confounded.
    May other gods themselves
    come to worship the true God.

8   May Zion hear of your judgements with joy,
    and the towns of Judah with gladness.

9   For you, Lord, are far superior to anything on earth,
    you are higher than all the other gods.

10 All of you who love the Lord, hate what is evil.
    He preserves the lives of his followers,
    and frees them from the clutches of the wicked.

11 There is light for the just,
    and joy for the pure in heart.

12 Rejoice in the Lord, all whose hearts are right,
    and give thanks to God for his holiness.

Psalm 98

Sing a new song to the Lord, the King

1   O sing a new song to the Lord,
    for he has done amazing things.
    With his right hand and holy arm

	he has won the victory.
2	The Lord has revealed his salvation to all— he has openly displayed his righteousness to the nations.
3	And to the house of Israel he also showed his tender love and mercy, so that his salvation is evident, even to the ends of the earth.
4	Make a joyful noise before the Lord, all the earth. Sing glad songs of joy and praise.
5	With instruments and voices raised in joyful melody, sing to the Lord.
6	With trumpets and horns, make a loud noise before the Lord, the King.
7	May this extend to the roaring of the sea, and all that is in it, to the ends of the earth, and all who live in it.
8	May the rivers join by clapping in rhythm, and the mountains add their happy sound.
9	For the Lord is coming— he is coming to judge the earth. He will judge all people in the right way, the way of justice.

Psalm 99

Praise our mighty God

1, 2   The Lord reigns—he is high above all people,
enthroned among the awesome creatures of heaven.
Tremble all people!
Quake all earth!

3   Praise his great and mighty name,
for the Lord is holy.

4   His strength lies in his just rule.
He loves justice and rules in righteousness.

5   All of you, exalt the Lord our God—
bow before him in worship, for he is holy.

6   Moses and Aaron were among his priests,
Samuel among those who called out to him.
They called out to the Lord
and he answered them.

7   He spoke to them in the pillar of cloud.
They kept his decrees and the law that he gave them.

8   It was you, O Lord, who answered them,
and tolerated their ways,
although when they went astray
you called them to book.

9   Come and worship God at his holy hill,
and hold him up high,
for the Lord our God is holy.

Psalm 100

All people that on earth do dwell, sing to the Lord with cheerful voice

1, 2   Come together, people of the earth!
Sing loud and joyful songs of praise to God.
Let your voices ring around the world,
and all that lives join in your heart-felt praise.

3   Acknowledge that we did not make ourselves,
The Lord is God, and he made everyone.
He is our shepherd, and we are his flock.
He cares for us, knows each of us by name.

4   Bring your joyful praise—enter his gates,
pass through his courts—
and give your thanks to God.
For God is good and God is love, give praise.
And God is faithful, God is true, give thanks.

5   His mercy and his truth will long endure,
His faithfulness for those yet to be born.

Psalm 101

*An individual chooses to do what is right
and to actively work against evil people*

1   O Lord, I want to sing a song to you,
I want to sing of love and justice.

2   My wish is to behave wisely,
and with integrity.
Will you be with me to help?
Even at home I want to be single-minded,
right to the depths of my heart.

3   I will not even look at anything that resembles evil.
    I hate the actions of those who forsake your way.
    They have no place near me.

4   Those with wayward hearts have left me,
    and any person who contemplates evil has departed.

5   All who slander their neighbor behind their backs,
    I will silence,
    and those who are arrogant and haughty,
    I will not tolerate.

6   I will only allow the faithful of the land
    to come into my house,
    only those who lead blameless lives
    to work for me.

7   The deceitful will not live where I live,
    nor the liar spend time with me.

8   Every morning I will silence all the wicked,
    and prevent them from entering
    the city of the Lord.

Psalm 102

A plea to the Lord from one in distress and alone

1   Listen to my prayer, O Lord,
    accept my cry for help.

2   Do not turn your back on me
    when I am in trouble.
    Bend your ear to me
    and be quick to respond.

3   My days are dissipating like smoke,
    and my bones burn like wood in the fire.

4   My heart is withered like grass and broken in half—
    I even forget to eat.

5   I am so emaciated with groaning,
    that I am just skin and bones.

6, 7	Alone, like a pelican in the wilderness, an owl in the desert, or like a lone sparrow on the rooftop, I wait and watch.
8	My enemies curse me all day long, and those who are angry with me, spread lies about me.
9, 10	Bread tastes like ashes to me, and my drink is diluted with tears, all because of your anger, for you lifted me up and now you have dropped me.
11	My days are like a fading shadow, and I wither like grass,
12	While you, O Lord, will endure forever, and memory of you through all generations.
13*	You will arise and be gracious to Zion, For the time to favor her, yes, the right time has come.
14	All your servants find pleasure even in her stones, and merit even in her dust.
15	Other nations will likewise come to be in awe of you, Lord. and all the kings of earth will bow down before your glory.
16	The Lord will come to restore Zion, and will be seen in full glory.
17	God will acknowledge the prayer of the desolate, and not ignore it.
18	The generations yet to be will read about this, and the people yet to be born will all praise the Lord.

---

* Verses 13 to 22—This section on Zion was probably added later. It is strange in an individual lament.

19   For the Lord looked down from heaven,
     observing the earth from there.

20   God heard the groaning of the prisoner,
     and freed even those on death-row.

21   God's name will be declared in Zion,
     God's glory praised in Jerusalem,

22   When all the people assemble,
     and every nation serves the Lord.

23   The Lord gave me an illness that made me weak,
     and threatened to shorten my days.

24   I prayed, O Lord, do not take me now,
     in the middle of life,
     while your days last forever.

25   Many ages ago you set the earth's foundation,
     and laid out the heavens.

26   Even though they may disappear,
     you will still be here.
     If they become worn out,
     you will change them like a piece of clothing.

27   Yet you will remain the same,
     year after year, for ever and ever.

28   And the children of those who serve you now,
     will still be here to love and serve you.

Psalm 103

*Calling on all creation to give thanks to God
for protection and care*

1   Bless the Lord, O my soul!
     From the depths of my being,

	I bless God's holy name.
2	Bless the Lord, O my soul!
	Never forget what he has done for me.
3–5	God forgives all our sins, heals us,
	and saves us from disaster.
	God gives us all we need and more,
	so that we are constantly renewed like an eagle,
	and he crowns it all
	with his tender love and mercy.
6	The Lord sees that there is justice
	for those suffering under oppression.
7	The Lord let Moses know his ways,
	and showed the children of Israel
	what he could do.
8	The Lord is full of mercy and grace,
	slow to anger and overflowing with love.
9	When the Lord does get angry,
	he does not hold onto it.
10	He has not punished us for our sins,
	nor repaid us for our wrongdoing as we deserve.
11	For as great as the distance is between heaven and earth,
	so great is the mercy
	God pours on those who revere him.
12	As great as the distance is between east and west,
	so far has he removed our sins from us.
13	As a parent tolerates his children's failures,
	so the Lord does those who worship him.
14–16	He knows all about us humans,
	understands how our minds work,
	remembers full well that we are made from dust.
	We are like any field-grass or wildflower—
	we appear, flourish,
	then we wither and are gone,
	as though we never were.

Psalm 104

17, 18   God's mercy, on the other hand,
to those who worship him,
to those who honor his covenant
and not only remember his commandments,
but obey them,
is from everlasting to everlasting,
and his righteousness,
from generation to generation.

19   The throne of the Lord is in heaven,
and from there he rules over all.

20   Bless the Lord, all you his angels,
whose strength lies in listening
to the word of the Lord,
and carrying it out.

21   Bless the Lord, all you his messengers,
all who minister for him,
all who carry out God's will.

22   Bless the Lord, all of God's creation,
in all places where he rules.
Bless the Lord, O my soul!

Psalm 104

A celebration of God's power over creation and God's providence

1, 2   My whole being, bless the Lord!
O Lord my God, you are so great—
honor and majesty are your clothing,
and light is wrapped around you as a cloak.
The heavens form the ceilings of your house,

3   your lofts are stored with water.
The clouds are your chariot,
and you are lifted up on the wings of the wind.

4	Your messengers are the winds, your ministers flaming fires.
5	You laid the foundations of the earth, making sure they held firm forever.
6	You covered it all with water— the waters so deep they cloaked the mountains.
7, 8	Then you gave the word of command and they fled, rushing down from the mountains, filling the valleys, until they reached the boundaries you determined.
9	The waters are bound by these limits, never again to cover all the earth.
10	Lord, you caused springs to flow in the valleys, so that their waters ran among the hills.
11	This provided drink for all the animals, allowing even the wild ass to quench his thirst.
12	Birds build their nests along the streams, singing in the branches of the trees.
13	You water the hills from your storehouses above, leaving the earth satisfied with your handiwork.
14	You, O Lord, make grass to grow as food for cattle, and you give us humans grain and plants for our own food.
15	You also gave us wine to bring joy to our hearts, oil for our enhancement, and bread to strengthen us.
16	You, Lord, planted trees like the cedars of Lebanon, which you water abundantly.
17	The birds nest in them. You also planted cypresses for the stork to build its nest.

Psalm 104

18   Higher in the hills the wild deer find shelter,
and the dassies a home.

19, 20   You gave us the moon to mark the seasons,
the setting of the sun, to bring on darkness.
This gives us night
when the creatures of the forest roam at large.

21   The young lions hunt for prey,
searching for the meat that you provide.

22   Then when the sun rises, they melt away,
to settle in their dens for the day.

23   That is when we humans awake for our work
and labor till nightfall.

24   O Lord, how varied is your creation—
all of it fashioned by you in wisdom.
The earth is full of your bounty.

25   The sea also, immense, and wide,
teams with your creation—
small beasts and large.

26   The ships sail on it.
They pass the whales,
who regard it as a playground.

27   All, all depend on you,
to give them their food
when it is needed.

28   When you are generous
they get enough and plenty,

29   When you no longer smile on them
they are in trouble.
When you take their breath away,
they die and return to dust.

30   When you send your spirit
new creatures come into being.
You renew the face of the earth.

| 31 | Your glory, Lord, will endure forever.
You take great pleasure in your work. |
|---|---|
| 32 | You only have to look on the earth
and it trembles,
touch the hills, and they smoke. |
| 33 | I will sing to my God as long as I have breath,
sing praises to my Lord as long as I live. |
| 34 | Meditating on God is a pleasure to me.
I find my joy in the Lord. |
| 35 | May all sinners be removed from the earth—
may the wicked cease to exist.
Bless the Lord, all my being!
Bless the Lord! |

Psalm 105

*Calling on people to praise God by retelling the history
of the Israelites up to their settlement in Canaan*

| 1 | O give thanks to the Lord!
Call out his name.
Broadcast his actions among all nations. |
|---|---|
| 2 | Sing to him, sing songs of praise,
telling of the amazing things he has done. |
| 3 | Give glory to his holy name.
Let the hearts of those
who look for God rejoice. |
| 4 | Search for the Lord and his strength,
long constantly for his presence. |
| 5 | Remember his wonderful deeds,
his miracles, and his judgements, |

Psalm 105

6   You children of Abraham and Sarah,
Jacob and Rachel, his servants whom he chose.

7   He is the Lord your God.
He judges the whole earth.

8   He remembers his covenant for ever—
his commandments that he formulated
for a thousand generations.

9   The covenant that he made with Abraham,
the promise he swore to Isaac,

10   Which he later confirmed in a decree to Jacob,
and sealed with Israel as an everlasting covenant.

11   It declared "I will give the land of Canaan to you,
as part of your inheritance."

12   This was when they were but few in number,
and strangers in the land.

13   When they roamed from nation to nation,
and kingdom to kingdom.

14   He allowed no-one to harm them.
He warned kings

15   "Do not even touch my anointed,
and do not harm my prophets."

16   He then imposed a famine on the land,
and disrupted the daily round of bread.

17   But he sent a man in preparation—
Joseph, who was sold as a slave,

18   His feet painfully shackled,
his neck in an iron collar.

19   He was tried by the Lord,
until the right time came.

20   The king himself released him,
the ruler of the people set him free.

21	He made him lord of his household,
	and put him in charge of all he owned.
22	He was to instruct his officials,
	and teach his elders wisdom.

23	Then Joseph's family came into Egypt,
	Jacob and his offspring came to stay.
24	The Lord increased them in number
	and they became too numerous
	for their oppressors.
25	God turned the hearts of the Egyptians against his people,
	so that they treated them shabbily.
26	Then the Lord sent them Moses, his servant,
	and Aaron, chosen to help.
27	They showed God's miraculous signs to the people,
	and worked wonders in the land of Ham.
28	God sent darkness, utter darkness,
	but the Egyptians did not see God in this.
29	God turned their water into blood,
	so that all the fish died.
30	Next, their land teemed with frogs,
	so many that they even invaded
	the living-quarters of the king.
31	God spoke again, and from the coast inland
	all was covered in flies and lice.
32	God sent them hail instead of rain,
	and lightning which caused fires throughout the land.
33	He blighted their vines and fig trees,
	and toppled the trees along their coast.
34	He called up swarms of locusts,
	and countless grasshoppers.
35	Who devoured all the grain in the land,
	and all the fruit it had produced.

36	Finally God struck down all their first-born, the first-fruits of their virility.
37	Only then were his people free to leave— they departed with silver and gold, and among them was not one feeble person.
38	Egypt was glad to see the backs of them, for dread of them had fallen on all.
39	God spread a cloud to cover them, and gave a fire to light up the night.
40	When the people asked for it, he gave them quails, and the bread of heaven, to satisfy their hunger.
41	He split rocks and water gushed out, running in dry areas like rivers.
42	For the Lord did not forget the promise he made to Abraham his servant.
43	And he liberated his people with gladness— his chosen ones with joyous song.
44, 45	The Lord gave them the lands of the nonbelievers, that they had already fully developed, that they might live by his precepts, and keep his commandments. Praise be to the Lord!

Psalm 106

A retelling of the history of Israel's sins from their escape from Egypt

1   Praise the Lord! All of you,
Give God thanks, for he is good—
his love will last forever.

2   Who can put into words all the deeds of the Lord?
Who can fully praise him?

3   Happy are those who maintain justice—
whose actions are right.

4, 5   Lord, when you favor your people,
remember me also with favor,
and mark me out for rescue,
that I may share the good you give them,
rejoice in their joy,
and revel in your heritage.

6   We have been sinful though,
and like our forebears,
we have turned shamelessly
in the wrong direction.

7   Our ancestors did not understand
how wonderful you were to them in Egypt,
and again, at the Reed Sea,
where already, they rebelled against you.

8   But for the sake of your reputation,
that your great power might become known,
you rescued them.

9   You issued a command to the Sea of Reeds,
that it be dry, and you led them through,
as though it were a desert.

10   So the Lord saved them
from the hand of their oppressors—
set them free from their enemy.

Psalm 106

11 The waters then rushed back
and drowned all their pursuers,
every last one!

12 That was when they all believed in God
and sang his praise.

13 But how soon after that
they forgot what God had done,
and rejected any advice of his.

14 They complained bitterly in the desert,
and tried God to the limit.

15 He gave in to their desires,
but it resulted in an emptiness in their soul.

16 They resented the position that Moses held among them,
and Aaron, who was consecrated to the Lord.

17 The earth opened and swallowed up Dathan,
and buried the group around Abiram.

18 Then a fire broke out in their midst
and the flames consumed the wicked.

19 This did not stop them.
They made a molded image to worship—
a golden calf, in Horeb.

20 Doing this brought down the glory of their god
to the level of an ox, chewing grass.

21, 22 They forgot the God who saved them
with great deeds in Egypt,
amazing miracles in the land of Ham
and awesome things at the Reed Sea.

23 In his anger God wanted to destroy them all
and he would have, had it not been for Moses,
who stood in the breach, and pleaded on their behalf.

24, 25 Then they did not believe God's word
about the land he promised,
nor would they do what he asked,

but grumbled to one another in their tents.

26 So God raised his hand to put an end to them,
while they were still in the wilderness,

27 Intending to scatter their offspring
among the nations,
like seed is scattered on the land.

28 They joined the worshippers of the Baal of Peor,
eating sacrifices made to dead gods.

29 They angered the Lord further
with their outrageous actions,
so he sent the plague among them.

30 At this point Phinehas stood up
and interceded for them,
and the plague ended.

31 This was credited to him as righteousness
from then on through all generations.

32 Yet again they made God angry—
this time at the waters of Meribah,
which caused Moses grief as well.

33 He became so disillusioned with them
that he said things he later regretted.

34 This was the time they would not destroy completely
the peoples whose land they occupied,
as God had commanded them.

35 Instead they lived among these nonbelievers
and copied their ways.

36-38 They became ensnared in
the worship of their idols.
even sacrificing their children to them.
They shed the blood of their children,
innocent blood, to local idols
and this blood polluted the land.

39 Their own actions condemned them.
   Their own lusts turned them into prostitutes.

40 This angered the Lord so much
   that he came to abhor his own people.

41 He handed them over to other nations
   who became their rulers,
   and held them in scant regard.

42 Other enemies also oppressed them,
   and they became captives in their own land.

43 This happened time and again—
   God would deliver them
   and they would forsake him.

44 Nevertheless he responded to their cries
   when they were distressed.

45 He was the one who held to the covenant
   and made allowances for them
   because of his abundant mercy.

46 He made them a cause of pity
   to those who captured them.

47 O Lord our God, save us!
   Gather our scattered people together again,
   so that we can give you thanks
   and praise your holy name.

48 Blessed be the Lord God of Israel
   who was, from before time began,
   and will be, when it comes to an end.
   Let all the people join in with a heartfelt
   AMEN.
   All of you! Praise the Lord!

BOOK V

Psalms 107–150

Psalm 107

Calling all people to give thanks and praise to the Lord

1. O give thanks to the Lord
   for he is good!
   His love will last forever.

2. Let those the Lord has saved join in—
   those he has rescued from the enemy,

3. And brought together from all over the world,
   from east and west, north and south.

4. Some of them had been wandering aimlessly
   in the desert, looking for a place to stay,

5. Hungry and thirsty,
   they were at their wits' end.

6. Then in their agony,
   they cried out to God,
   and he came to their aid,

7. Putting them on the right road,
   that led to help and home.

8. *O that all people would
   praise the Lord for his goodness—
   for his wonderful actions
   on their behalf.*

Psalm 107

9   For he is the one who gives
the searching soul satisfaction,
and the hungry soul the nourishment it needs.

10, 11   Others were on the wrong path,
ending up bound in chains and irons,
facing darkness and death—
the result of rejecting the words of God,
and showing contempt
for the counsel of the God above all.

12   He brought them into hard labor,
and they ended up oppressed and without help.

13   They cried to the Lord then, in their trouble,
and he lifted them out of their agony and distress.

14   He broke their chains wide open,
And brought them out of darkness and
the prospect of death.

15   *O that all people would*
praise the Lord for his goodness—
for his wonderful actions
on their behalf.

16   For God has broken open the gates of bronze,
and snapped the bars of iron in half.

17   There were also the foolish ones,
who became ill through their own sins,

18   To the point that their bodies rejected food,
and they drew near to death.

19   They turned to the Lord in their trouble.
He heard them and lifted them out of their distress.

20   God bent down and healed them,
and set them free of their affliction.

21   *O that all people would*
praise the Lord for his goodness—
for his wonderful actions
on their behalf.

Psalm 107

22   Let all of them offer the sacrifices of thanksgiving,
     and tell of his actions with joy.

23   Yet other people ply their trade upon the seas,
     sailing over the waters.

24   These also see God at work,
     his miracles in the depths of the sea.

25   He gives the command, and the wind builds up—
     it whips up the waves in a fury,

26   Lifting any on the water up to the heavens,
     and then dropping them into the depths,
     making their hearts stand still.

27   They reel around,
     staggering like a drunkard,
     their own abilities stretched beyond limit.

28, 29   In their terror they cry out to the Lord,
     and he lifts them out of their distress,
     stilling the storm and restoring calm.

30   They rejoice in the stillness,
     and thankfully reach their chosen haven.

31   *O that all people would*
     praise the Lord for his goodness—
     for his wonderful actions
     on their behalf.

32   May all those gathered
     in the congregation of the people raise him high,
     and those in the council of the elders praise him.

33   He is the one who can turn rivers into a desert,
     and springs of water into dry ground.

34   A fruitful land can become barren
     if the inhabitants are full of evil.

35   He is also the one who can turn
     the desert into a lake,
     and dry land into springs of water,

36   Allowing the hungry to settle there,
     build themselves a town to live in,

37   Prepare the soil for crops,
     and plant vineyards that will yield copiously.

38   He gives them his blessing,
     so that they increase in number,
     along with their cattle.

39   On the other hand he can decrease their numbers,
     and increase their affliction and sorrow,
     and the oppression they suffer.

40   He can hold princes in contempt,
     and they will lose their way
     in the wilderness,

41   But the poor he will always lift up
     out of their suffering,
     and their families will flourish.

42   The righteous will take note and rejoice.
     Evildoers will have nothing to say.

43   So take note of these things,
     live them out,
     and you will come to know intimately
     the compassion of the Lord.

Psalm 108[*]

A plea with praise and assurance that God will help

1   O God, I will sing songs of praise to your glory.
    for my heart is at peace.

---

[*] Psalm 108 consists of two other sections of psalms which have been stitched together with a few variations, or all three may have been taken from an earlier poem. The reason is not known.

2	I will be awake early, so be awake as well, my lyre and harp.
3	I want my praise of God to reach all people.
4	For God's mercy is as high as the heavens, God's truth stretching way over the clouds.
5	O Lord, may you be held in honor higher than the heavens, and lifted up in glory far above the earth.
6	Answer me and come to my aid. Give me a hand to deliver me.
7	God had spoken in his holiness, "Gladly will I divide up Shechem, and share out the valley of Succoth.
8	Gilead belongs to me, as does Manasseh. Ephraim is my helmet, Judah my scepter.
9	Moab is my washbasin, on Edom I fling my sandal, over Philistia I exult in triumph."
10	Who is going to lead us into the fortified city? Who will lead us into Edom?
11	Will you, O God? Or have you indeed rejected us? Because you no longer go out with our army.
12	Give us your help against the enemy, because it is hopeless relying on other people.
13	But with God's help we will do valiantly, for he will trample down our enemies.

Psalm 109

*Catalogue of an individual being treated badly
and calling down a curse on his enemy*

1   O God, you are the one I praise!
       Do not be silent in response.

2   The wicked and the deceitful are not silent.
       Their voices are raised spreading lies about me.

3   Without any reason to do so,
       they have poured words of hate over me.

4   In return for my love, they take issue with me,
       although I pray for them.

5   They give me suffering in return for help,
       hate where I offer compassion.

6   They say to each other,
       "Let us send this unprincipled man after him,
       and this accuser to follow him."
       and then they curse me:

7   "In the courts may judgement go against him,
       and may his pleas not affect the guilty verdict.

8   May his days be few,
       and may someone else take his position.

9   Let his children be without a father,
       and his wife without a husband.

10   May his children end up as beggars,
       looking for bread on the dumps.

11   Let the crime boss take him to the cleaners,
       and let the immigrant take his job.

12   May there be not even one to show him any compassion,
       or to help his destitute children.

13   May his legacy be cut off,
       his name be as if it never was.

14	With the Lord may all the sins
	of his forefathers be remembered.
	May none of his foremothers' be washed away.
15	May God always be aware of their sins,
	so that all memory of them is wiped from the earth."
16	Rather, may all these curses
	fall on the heads of those who curse me—
	because the one against me showed no mercy,
	but pursued one who was poor and needy
	and broke his heart even more.
17	Where he spat out curses, may they all return to him.
	Where he showed no delight in blessing,
	may none come his way.
18	He wore cursing as he wears his clothes,
	may it enter his body like water,
	his bones like oil.
19	Let it become his clothing to cover him completely,
	and his belt to fasten around him at all times.
20	Let this be the reward from God to my enemies,
	and to those who say dreadful things about me.
21	But as for me, O Lord, because you are good,
	because it is in your nature,
	set me free from all of this.
22	For I am poor and needy
	and on top of that, heartbroken.
23	I have faded like a shadow at evening,
	been tossed about like leaves in the wind.
24	My legs are weak from fasting,
	and there is no longer any fat on my bones.
25	I have become an object of scorn to my enemies—
	when they see me, they shake their heads.

26   Help me, O Lord my God,
         take pity on me and save me.

27   May the enemy see you do it—
         may they know it is you who rescued me.

28   They may curse, but you bless.
         When they get up each morning,
         may it be to shame,
         but let your servant wake to joy.

29   Let those against me be covered
         as with a cloak, in shame,
         draped as with a shawl, in confusion.

30   I will raise my voice in praise to God, the Great,
         especially where crowds gather.

31   For God stands at the right-hand of the one in need,
         to save him from those who condemn him.

Psalm 110

A royal psalm—assuring the king of power with God on his side

1   The Lord said to my lord the king,
         "Sit on my right-hand side
         until I make your enemies your footstool."

2   The Lord will extend the sway of your powerful scepter,
         and from Zion you will rule over your enemies.

3   With God giving you the power,
         your people will rally to battle,
         when, in the dew of your youth, your force assembles
         on the holy mountain at dawn,

4   The Lord has promised with a mind that will not change,
         "You are a priest, and will be forever,
         according to my solemn word,
         O righteous king."

5   The Lord, who is on your right-hand,
        will strike down kings,
        if angry with them.

6   The Lord will be judge over the nonbelievers—
        the places of those condemned to death will be full.
        The leaders of many countries will be wounded.

7   You will drink water from the streams along the path,
        and so you will always have your head held high.

Psalm 111

An acrostic praise-song, listing God's attributes

1   Praise the Lord! Hallelujah!
        With my whole heart I will praise the Lord!
        I will praise the Lord in the congregation,
        in the assembly of the upright.

2   The Lord's actions are great,
        pondered with pleasure
        by those who look for them.

3   His actions are full of honor and majesty,
        and his generosity will live forever.

4   The Lord is full of grace and compassion—
        who can ever forget his wonderful deeds?

5   God provides sustenance to those who hold him in awe.
        He will never forget his covenant.

6   He showed his people his power in action,
        when he gave them the land
        belonging to other nations.

7   What he does with his hands is true and well-judged—
        what he commands with his lips is trustworthy.

8   These will stand firm for ever and ever –
    all carried out in a just and right way.

9   God set his people free—
    he set up a covenant with them that will last forever.

10 God's name is held above and beyond any other name.
    To fear the Lord is the first step to wisdom—
    to do what he commands the way to understanding.
    Praise the Lord forever!   Hallelujah!

Psalm 112

*Contrasting the fate of the righteous with the wicked
in a short acrostic poem*

1   Praise the Lord! Hallelujah!
    Happy are those who worship the Lord,
    who take great delight in his teaching.

2   Their families will be great on earth,
    and all their children will be blessed.

3   Their right actions will last forever
    and their houses be full of abundance and wealth.

4   The upright are gracious and compassionate.
    They do what is right in everything.
    Light glows from them, dispelling the darkness.

5   Those that are good are willing to lend.
    They conduct their affairs with integrity.

6   They will stand forever unshakable,
    and will never be forgotten.

7   Even bad news will not knock the upright off their feet,
    because their hearts are firm in trusting the Lord.

8   Their hearts will remain steadfast, and they will know no fear,
    until their enemies are conquered.

9   They have been generous, giving to the poor—
   their goodness will last forever,
   their strength be acknowledged with honor.

10   In contrast, the wicked will see it and rage,
   but their anger will come to nothing,
   their desires will all die.

Psalm 113*

Praise the Lord—who helps the lowly.

Hallelujah! Praise the Lord!

1   Praise the Lord, all you servants of the Lord,
   praise the name of the Lord!

2   May the name of the Lord be blessed
   now and forever.

3   From the rising of the sun to its setting,
   may the Lord's name be praised.

5   Who can we compare with the Lord our God?
   For our God is above all others.

4   Our God is above every nation,
   with glory that stretches above the heavens.

6   Yet with eyes that see what happens
   in heaven and on earth.

7   The Lord raises the poor out of the dust,
   and lifts the needy from the dump.

8   So that they may be found among princes,
   even the princes of their own people.

9   And the woman who was barren,
   is given a joyful house full of children.

---

* Psalm 113 is the first of six psalms of praise, Ps 113 to 118, known as the "hallel", a word meaning "praise".

Praise the Lord!
Hallelujah!

Psalm 114

The earth is affected by God's actions, an acrostic Psalm.

1. When Israel escaped from Egypt,
   the house of Jacob from people
   who spoke in a barbaric tongue,

2. The land of Judah became God's sanctuary,
   the land of Israel God's domain.

3. When the Sea saw this it withdrew,
   and the River Jordan was driven back.

4. The mountains skipped like rams,
   the hills frolicked like lambs.

5. What caused you, O Sea, to withdraw?
   and you River, what drove you back?

6. Why did you skip like rams, O Mountains?
   and you Hills, why did you frolic like lambs?

7. Tremble, O Earth, at the presence of the Lord,
   at the presence of the God of Jacob and Rachel.

8. The Lord is the one who can turn the rock into a pool,
   flint into a fountain of water.

Psalm 115

Our God is alive, unlike hand-made idols

1. Not to us, O Lord, not to us,
   give glory, but to your name,
   for your mercy and faithfulness.

2	Why do the heathen ask, "Where is their god?"
3	For you, our God, are in the heavens, and you can do whatever you want.
4	Their gods are only idols, made of silver or gold— fashioned by human hands.
5	They have eyes, but no sight, mouths, but no speech.
6	They have ears that do not hear, noses that cannot smell.
7	They have hands, but cannot feel, Feet, but cannot walk. They cannot utter one word through their throats.
8	Their makers are much like them, as are all those who put their trust in them.
9	O people of Israel, trust in the Lord. The Lord is your help and your protection.
10	O people of Aaron, trust in the Lord. The Lord is your help and your protection.
11	All you who worship the Lord, trust in the one who is your help and your protection.
12	The Lord keeps us in mind, to bless us with rich blessings for the people of Israel, as well as the people of Aaron.
13	The Lord will bless all those who worship honestly, whether important or not.
14	The Lord will see that you increase in number, you and your children.
15	The Lord who made heaven and earth will bless you.

16   The heavens belong to the Lord,
   but the earth has been entrusted to our care.

17   Those who go down into the place of silence—
   those who have died, can no longer praise the Lord.

18   But we will bless the Lord,
   now and forevermore.

Psalm 116

Thanksgiving of an individual for delivery from near death

1   I love the Lord,
   because he heard my voice,
   and my prayers for mercy.

2   He turned his ear towards my voice,
   when I called to him.

3   I found myself in trouble,
   death circling around me—
   the pains of Sheol had me in their grip,
   filling me with sorrow.

4   Then I called on the Lord,
   "O Lord, I plead with you. Save my life!"

5   Our Lord is gracious and just,
   and full of compassion.

6   He looks after even the simplest person.
   He helped me when I was at the lowest point.

7   Our Lord treated me generously,
   restoring my peace of mind.

8   He delivered my life from death,
   my eyes from tears, and my feet from tripping up.

9   I will walk with the Lord
   in the land of the living.

10   I believed, but my illness tested me sorely—
11   I came close to saying that it was all a lie.
12   What can I give back to the Lord,
     for all his gifts to me?
13   I will accept the cup of salvation he offers,
     I will call on him from now on.
14   I will carry out the vows I made to the Lord
     in front of everyone.
15   The Lord puts great value
     on the death of any of his devoted ones.
16   O Lord, you have untied the knots that bound me.
     I am truly your servant, as my mother was before me.
17   I will bring my offering of thanksgiving to you.
     I will call on your name.
18   I will carry out the vows I made to the Lord
     in front of everyone,
19   In the house of the Lord,
     in the center of Jerusalem.
     Praise the Lord! Hallelujah!

Psalm 117

The shortest praise song, encompassing all people

1   Praise the Lord! All nations of the world!
    Praise the Lord, all people!
2   The Lord's compassion for us
    is great beyond measure.
    The Lord's faithfulness endures forever.
    Praise the Lord!

Psalm 118

*O give thanks to the Lord, for God's love will last forever,
and God will give you victory*

1. O give thanks to the Lord, for he is good.
   God's love will last forever.

2. Let Israel now say,
   God's love will last forever.

3. Let the house of Aaron now say,
   God's love will last forever.

4. Let those who worship the Lord now say,
   God's love will last forever.

5. I called on the Lord when I was in distress—
   the Lord answered me and lifted me to a stress-free place.

6. The Lord is on my side, so I will not be afraid.
   What can a mere mortal do to me?

7. The Lord takes the side of my supporters,
   so I shall see my detractors defeated.

8. It is better to put your trust in the Lord
   than in any other person.

9. It is better to put your trust in the Lord,
   than to rely even on princes.

10. If every other nation besieged me,
    in the name of the Lord, I would overcome them.

11. They may besiege me, they may fully encircle me,
    but in the Lord's name I will destroy them.

12. They may swarm over me like a hive of bees,
    but they will be extinguished
    as bees are with a burning branch of thorns.

13. They attacked me with such vigor,
    determined to bring me down,
    but the Lord saved me.

PSALM 118

14 The Lord is my strength and my song,
    giving me the victory!

15 There are songs of victory and joy in the
    houses of the upright.
    The Lord's right hand rescued them all.

16 The right hand of the Lord gave the V-sign for victory—
    the right hand of the Lord won the day.

17 Now I shall not die, but live
    to tell others about the way the Lord works.

18 The Lord may have put me through the wringer,
    but he did not let me die.

19, 20 Open for me the gate to the right way of living,
    and I will enter, praising the Lord,
    for the gate to the right way of life, the Lord's gate,
    is the one to enter.

21 The stone which the builders rejected,
    has now become the cornerstone of the building.

22 It is the Lord's doing,
    and is wonderful in our eyes.

24 This is the day when the Lord will act—
    we will rejoice and be glad in it.

25 Lord, we implore you, save us now,
    and help us to flourish.

26 May the one coming to us
    in your name, Lord, be blessed.
    He will be blessed indeed from your house.

27 O God, you are the Lord who gives us light,
    so we bring leafy branches
    and in procession adorn your altar.

28 Lord, you are my God, and I want to praise you!
    You are my God and I want to exalt you!

29 Lord, I give you thanks, for you are good,
    Your love will last forever.

Psalm 119[*]

*A teaching psalm of devotion to the "way of the Lord",
that is, to God's "law" or "teaching"*

Aleph

1. All those who keep walking
   in the way of the Lord are happy indeed.

2. All those who do God's will
   and search for God whole-heartedly are happy indeed.

3. They are the ones who walk along God's path,
   doing no wrong.

4. God, you commanded us
   to keep your precepts diligently.

5. O God, I want to face in the right direction
   for keeping your rules.

6. Then, because I carry out all you want me to do,
   I will have no shame.

7. As I learn your way, the right way,
   I will have the right heart to praise you.

8. I want to stick to your decrees,
   so do not leave me to my own devises.

Beth

9. How can the young live clean lives?
   By following your word.

10. I have looked for you with my whole heart.

---

[*] Psalm 119 was written acrostically—each stanza of eight lines starting with a letter of the Hebrew alphabet in order. It is hard to maintain this in translation, but each stanza is headed with the appropriate letter.

The right ordering of life is found in "the way of the Lord", and in this long poem many synonyms are used for this. The most prominent are "the teaching" and the "torah" (the Law or laws).

Others, in translation into English are: command, decree, directive, direction, God's will, judgement, principle, revelation, rule, rule of life, standard, what is right, word.

Let me not wander from your way.

11. I have taken your word to heart,
that I do not act in any way against it.

12. You are very special, O Lord,
teach me your way of life.

13. I have voiced with my lips
all the judgements from your mouth.

14. I have been as glad of what you have revealed to me,
as though it were the finest of riches.

15. I will meditate on your teachings,
and respect your way.

16. I will take delight in your commands,
and remember your words.

Gimel

17. Treat your servant generously,
that I may live and keep your word.

18. Open my eyes, that I may see
the wonderful things that are in your law.

19. I feel I am a wanderer through the land,
looking for the hidden law of God,

20. Heart-sore with longing to find
your rulings on the way things should be.

21. Those who are too proud to follow your way
will be rebuked with a curse.

22. But I have kept to your way,
so keep me clear of reproach and condemnation.

23. Even though the corrupt bad-mouthed me,
I thought only of your laws.

24. Your revelations are my delight,
as they counsel me.

Daleth

25. When I feel down in the dumps,
    enliven me with your word.

26. I made clear the way I was taking—
    and you accepted me—now teach me your rules.

27. Help me to understand how your rule of life works,
    so that I can always bear in mind your wonders.

28. My soul is melting away in sorrow—
    let your word give me strength.

29. Take from me any deceitful way,
    and graciously give me your law.

30. I want to walk in the way of truth.
    That is why I have chosen to follow your laws.

31. I keep to what you have revealed to me.
    Do not let me be ashamed.

32. I will run after your commandments
    if you increase my understanding.

He

33. Every day, Lord, teach me your way of life,
    and I shall walk in it without fail.

34. Give me the inner knowledge to keep your law,
    and with all my heart I will do so.

35. Help me to walk in the path you have set out,
    and it shall be my delight to do so.

36. Let me strive after your revelations,
    and not my own gain.

37. Turn my eyes away from false pursuits,
    but let me come alive to your way.

38. I am devoted to your worship,
    so, as your servant, may it be my foundation.

39. I am afraid of being found wanting in your judgement,
    which is always good.

40   See how I long for your standards.
         Let your righteousness be born in me.

Waw

41   O Lord, send love and salvation to me,
         as your word promises.

42   I trust in your word—
         it will enable me to answer those who accuse me.

43   I have hope in what you judge to be true.
         Do not take this truth from me.

44   Then I will be able to keep your law
         for all time.

45   And I will walk free
         while I look for the way to embody your rule of life.

46   I will tell even the highest in the land what you reveal to me,
         without any shame.

47   I will find delight in your commandments,
         which are dear to me.

48   And my hands will carry out your commands which I love,
         and my mind meditate on them.

Zain

49   Bring to mind the word that you gave me—
         the word which gave me hope.

50   Your word gave me life,
         and comforted me when I was upset.

51   The arrogant deride me,
         yet I have not forsaken your law.

52   I have stood by the decisions I made long ago,
         and this has brought peace of mind,

53   Even though I have been horrified by the way
         wrongdoers ignore your commands.

54   Your laws have been the theme of
         the songs that I sing on my pilgrimage.

55 Day and night I remember your name, O Lord,
and have kept to your way.

56 And because of this,
you have given me your blessing.

Heth

57 Here I am, O Lord, having said
that I would keep your word.

58 Now I entreat you with my whole heart
to show me mercy as you have promised.

59 Having thought about the way I was headed,
I turned my feet in your direction.

60 I lost no time and was quick to
keep your commands.

61 Even though I was enticed away by wrongdoers,
I did not forsake your laws.

62 In the middle of the night
I will get up to give you thanks,
because your laws are so just.

63 I am in the company of all those
who worship you and keep to your ways.

64 The earth is full of your love, O Lord—
teach me all your rules of life.

Teth

65 I know, O Lord, that your word is good
and you have treated me in accordance with that.

66 Teach me more of your word in which I believe—
give me knowledge and good judgement.

67 Before I was convicted of my sin,
and brought low, I went astray,
but now I keep your word.

68 You are good, and you do good.
Teach me the way you want me to act.

69	Even though the arrogant have spread lies about me,
	I will still follow your way with my whole heart.
70	Their hearts are as slippery as grease,
	but I delight in keeping your law.
71	It was good for me to have been humbled
	so that I might turn and see your demands on me.
72	The word that comes from your mouth
	is better than any amount of silver or gold.

Yodh

73	Just as the hands that made me and molded me
	gave me a brain,
	may I use it to learn your commands.
74	Those who worship you will be glad to see
	that I also hope in your word.
75	I know, O Lord, that what you decide is right,
	and that you brought me low in good faith.
76	Now let your compassion comfort me,
	as your word to your servant promises.
77	Let me be filled with your tender love,
	which will restore my life, for I delight in your word.
78	Bring shame to those bent on wronging me for no reason,
	but keep me meditating on your words.
79	May I be supported by those who follow you,
	those who have known your revelations.
80	Let my heart become solidly grounded in your principles,
	so that I am not ashamed.

Kaph

81	My soul faints with longing for you to save me.
	I wait in hope for this.
82	My eyes strain to see your word come true,
	as I ask how soon you will come to comfort me.

83	I am ready to crack like heated glass,
	yet I do not forget your teaching.
84	How much longer must your servant wait
	before you pronounce my persecutors guilty.
85	The arrogant who have dug pits for me,
	are wrong to persecute me.
86	They are going against your laws which are all just.
	Help me, I pray.
87	They almost ended my days on earth,
	but I still kept to your teaching.
88	In your compassion, restore my life
	so that I can keep doing what you have shown me.

Lamedh

89	Lord our God, your word is secure in heaven for evermore.
90	In the earth, which you established,
	your faithfulness encompasses all generations.
91	Heaven and earth will continue to function
	according to laws you set for all.
92	If I had not found that I delighted to keep your law
	I would have succumbed to my pain.
93	I will always remember your rule of life,
	because it gives me life indeed.
94	I am yours. Save me.
	I have never forgotten your teaching.
95	The wicked have tried to destroy me,
	but I stick to your principles.
96	Even if things on earth were perfect,
	your law would exceed them all in perfection, O God.

Mem

| 97 | My meditation every day is on your law. |
| | I love it dearly. |

| 98 | You have made me wiser than my enemies
| | through your teaching,
| | for it is always with me.

| 99 | Because your teaching is what I meditate on,
| | I now understand more than all my teachers.

| 100 | Because I live by your principles,
| | I understand more than the wise of old.

| 101 | And because I keep your word,
| | I have kept my feet from walking in the wrong direction.

| 102 | I have not deviated from your judgements,
| | for you have been my teacher.

| 103 | How sweet the taste of your words,
| | sweeter to my tongue even than honey.

| 104 | I grow in understanding through your teaching—
| | that is why I hate every way that is false.

Nun

| 105 | Nothing lights my way like your word—
| | it is a lamp guiding my footsteps.

| 106 | I have promised, and I mean it,
| | that I will stick to your good judgements.

| 107 | I am in great pain, O Lord,
| | give your word and restore my life,

| 108 | Accept my promises freely given,
| | and give me further teaching.

| 109 | My soul is at risk all the time,
| | but I never forget your word.

| 110 | The wicked tried to snare me.
| | Nevertheless, I remained obedient to your commands.

| 111 | What you show me gives me deep-down joy.
| | It will remain my heritage forever.

| 112 | My heart is set on living by your principles,
| | right through to the end.

Samekh

113   O Lord, I hate trivial thoughts,
       but I love your words.

114   You are my hiding-place, and my stronghold—
       your word gives me hope.

115   Leave me alone, wrongdoers,
       for I want to do God's will.

116   O God, fortify me by your word,
       so that I may live unashamed of my hope.

117   Keep me safe from falling,
       so that I continually carry out your will.

118   You have kept down all those
       who do not follow your law—
       those who deceive with their lies.

119   You discard all the wicked of the earth as dross,
       but I love your way of life.

120   I tremble before you,
       I am apprehensive as to how you will judge my life.

Ain

121   Protect me from my oppressors,
       for I have been good and just.

122   Do not let the arrogant lord it over me,
       vouchsafe the good in me
       when they oppress me.

123   My eyes fail with looking for your saving grace,
       my ears with waiting to hear
       your word of righteousness.

124   Treat your servant with pity,
       and teach me your rule of life.

125   I am your servant.
       Give me a mind that understands,
       for I wish to know all your laws.

126 Now is the right time for you to act, O Lord,
for they have made a mockery of your whole law.

127 I, though, love your commandments more than gold,
more even than the most refined gold.

128 I consider all your commandments as true and right.
I hate every other way, for they are all false.

Pe

129 Your word is wonderful—
I want to make it all my own.

130 When your word enters the soul it lights it up.
It brings new understanding to the simple.

131 I long for your way of life
as one panting with open mouth.

132 Look on me with pity,
as it is in your nature to look
on those who love you.

133 Help me order my steps to follow your word,
so that sin no longer dictates their direction.

134 Help me also to be free
of the oppressing influence of others—
I want to stick to your rules.

135 Smile upon me, O Lord.
Teach me your way.

136 When your law is flouted
I weep rivers of tears.

Tzade

137 You are the righteous one, O Lord.
Your rulings are just.

138 The laws you gave us are right and just.

139 I get consumed with agitation
when your word is ignored
and your laws broken.

140 Your word is full of integrity.
    I, your servant, love it all.

141 Small and despised though I may be,
    I aim to keep each word.

142 Your righteousness will last forever.
    Your law is truth.

143 Trouble and sorrow may overwhelm me,
    yet I will still find delight in your rules of life.

144 Your directives are right and will last forever.
    Help me to understand them and I shall have life.

Qoph

145 My whole being cried out to you,
    "Lord, hear me!" for I keep your commands,

146 I cried, "Save me!" for I always obey your directives.

147 I cried so much that dawn never seemed to come,
    saying, "I wait for your word."

148 Through the night hours I look to you,
    meditating on your promises.

149 In your loving kindness, O Lord, hear my voice.
    In your love of justice, restore my life.

150 Those who are up to no good are drawing closer—
    they care nothing for your law.

151 Yet you are near, O Lord.
    All your laws are true indeed.

152 All along I have known that your
    Law will last forever,
    because it was established
    before time began.

Resh

153 Think of my suffering and free me from it,
    for I have not forgotten your law.

154	Take up my cause and free me.
	Give me life again in line with your word.
155	Salvation is far from the wicked.
	They are not looking for your way of life.
156	Your tender kindnesses are great.
	May your decision be to give me back my life.
157	My enemies and persecutors may be many,
	yet I never deviate from following your commands,
158	It grieved me to see those who broke your laws,
	and ignored your word.
159	As befits your love, give me life—
	See how I love to do your will.
160	The essence of your word is truth—
	the result of your judgement is justice.

Shin

161	I have been persecuted by rulers for no reason,
	but this has not stopped me
	from worshipping your word.
162	I rejoice in your word,
	as I would over finding great treasure.
163	I love your teaching,
	just as I hate and deplore lying.
164	I stop to praise you seven times each day
	because your laws are so just.
165	Those who love your law find a deep peace,
	so that nothing disturbs them.
166	Lord, I have kept your commandments,
	and my hope is that you will save me.
167	From deep within my heart I love your principles,
	and have kept to them.
168	I have acted as you would wish,
	as you can clearly see.

PSALM 120

Tau

169   May my cry to you come within earshot, O Lord.
May I understand your word.

170   May you hear my plea, and free me—
you gave your word.

171   Let my lips give voice to my praise,
once you have taught me your rule of life.

172   Let my tongue give voice to your word,
because all your rules of life are good and right.

173   May you always give me a helping hand,
for I have chosen to follow your way.

174   I have longed to be kept safe
while on your way, O Lord,
for I delight in keeping your law.

175   Let my soul be alive,
and let your principles guide me,
so that I can live a life of praise.

176   If ever I should stray like a lost sheep,
look for me and look after me,
for I never want to abandon your way of life.

Psalm 120*

I am the only one for peace

1, 2   When I was in distress I cried to the Lord,
asking to be saved from lying lips
and a deceitful tongue.
The Lord heard my prayer.

---

* Psalm 120 is the first of fifteen psalms (Pss 120–34) which together form the Great Hallel (Hymn of Praise) Each also bears the title, *A song of ascents*. Its actual meaning is disputed. These psalms are generally considered to have been composed in the post-Exilic period.

3	What can be done about the false tongue?
4	It is like sharpened arrows, like burning coals of the broom bush.
5	Whether I live, a foreigner, in Mesech or near the tents of Kedar,
6	I would still live too close among those who hate peace.
7	I am for peace and would talk about that— they are all for war.

Psalm 121

Does help come from the hills?

1	I will lift up my eyes to look at the hills, but does my help come from there?
2	No, it comes from the Lord, who made heaven and earth.
3	The Lord is the one who guards you, and will not let you stumble, because there is no sleeping on the job.
4	Indeed, the one who guards our land neither sleeps nor takes a nap.
5	It is the Lord who guards you— who is the shade on your right side,
6	To prevent the sun from overpowering you by day, and the moon by night.
7	The Lord will protect you from any harm and will guard your life.
8	The Lord will guard all your activities, whether you go out or stay in, from now and forever.

Psalm 122

May peace come to Jerusalem—a personal plea

1   I rejoiced with those who said to me,
         "Let us go to God's house."

2   Our feet have entered your gates,
         O Jerusalem.

3   Jerusalem, a city built compactly,
         built for God.

4   To you come the various people of the Lord –
         the people of Israel
         to give thanks to our Lord.

5   For here were established the courts of law,
         and here began the rule of the house of David.

6   May all pray for your peace, O Jerusalem,
         that those who love you may flourish.

7   Pray that peace may reign within your walls,
         and prosperity within your houses.

8   For the sake of my family and friends, I repeat.
         "May peace come to Jerusalem!"

9   I will pray the greatest blessing for you,
         for within your walls
         is the house of our God.

Psalm 123

A prayer, both personal and communal, for help when being scorned

1   I raise my eyes to gaze on you, O Lord,
         you, whose throne is in heaven.

2   As the eyes of a servant follow the hand of his master
    and the eyes of a serving-maid that of her mistress,
    we all turn our gaze on you,
    and wait for you, O God, to turn to us
    and show us your mercy.

3   Have mercy on us.
    Have mercy on us all, O Lord,

4   For we are being subjected to a deluge of contempt,
    an outpouring of scorn from the arrogant,
    who sit at ease with nothing better to do.

Psalm 124

Praise to God for rescue from the enemy

1   If it had not been that the Lord was on our side—
    Israel can now say—

2   If the Lord had not been on our side
    when we were attacked,

3   Then our attackers, so full of aggression,
    would easily have swallowed us alive.

4   Like floods, they would have poured over us,
    engulfing us way past our necks.

5   Like rushing waters,
    they would have swept us away.

6   Praise be to our Lord,
    who did not let them get their teeth into us.

7   We have escaped like a bird flying free
    through a tear in the catcher's net.

8   Our help came from the Lord our God,
    creator of heaven and earth.

Psalm 125

Zion as the believer's solid ground

1. Those who trust in the Lord
   are as firm as Mount Zion—
   unmovable, standing forever.

2. The Lord encircles his people
   and always will,
   as the mountains surround Jerusalem.

3. The spirit of evil will not hover
   over the lands given to those who are good,
   so that they will not be influenced
   to do wrong.

4. Be good, O Lord, to those who are good,
   and have integrity of heart.

5. But may you banish with the evildoers
   those who deviate from your way.

Psalm 126

Sow in sorrow, reap in joy

1. When the Lord restored the fortunes of Zion,
   it was like a dream become reality.

2. Laughter filled the air.
   Joy broke into song.
   The nations said to one another,
   "The Lord has done great things for them."

3. The Lord had done great things for us
   and we celebrated.

4   As the watercourses in the Negev
    flow with water after rain,
    so the Lord restored life in Jerusalem,
    and filled our hearts with joy.

5   Those who sow with tears of sorrow,
    will reap with shouts of joy.

6   Yes, those who go out to sow with heavy hearts,
    will harvest their grain with songs of joy.

Psalm 127

Put the Lord in charge

1   Unless the Lord is in charge,
    you will labor in vain to build your house.
    Unless the Lord watches over your city,
    the guards will watch over it in vain.

2   Rise early, work all day, stay up late—
    if it is all for other "gods",
    it is all in vain.
    The Lord will provide for his beloved.

3   Children may be the fruit of the womb,
    but they come to you as a gift from the Lord.

4   Children that are given to those still young
    are like weapons in the hands of the strong.

5   Happy are the parents who have a house full of them.
    They will be able to negotiate from a position of power
    with their adversaries.

Psalm 128

Peace and prosperity to those who worship God

1. Those who worship and walk along the path with God,
   are the happy ones.

2. They will experience the reward that labor brings.
   They will know well-being.

3. Their spouses will be fruitful like vines
   growing up the sides of their houses,
   their children like olive trees
   around their dwellings.

4. This is the blessing that comes
   to those who worship the Lord.

5. May the God of Zion bless you.
   May you enjoy the prosperity of Jerusalem
   all your days.

6. May you live to see your grandchildren,
   and may peace envelop Israel.

Psalm 129

Affirming how the Lord saved Israel and a curse on her enemies

1. "Many a time since my youth," Israel can now say,
   "I have been attacked."

2. Yes, many a time from early on
   enemies have attacked her,
   yet they never conquered her.

3. The ploughers ploughed right across her back,
   making long furrows,

4. But the Lord, the righteous one,
   slashed her bonds.

| 5 | May all those who hate Zion
    be overcome and forced to retreat. |
|---|---|
| 6 | Let them be like grass sprouting on roofs—
    it withers even before it starts to grow. |
| 7 | It would yield nothing if it were harvested,
    nothing to bind into sheaves. |
| 8 | Let no one passing by offer them God's blessing—
    no-one say, "We bless you in the name of the Lord." |

Psalm 130

Longing for the Lord, out of the depths

| 1 | Out of the depths
    I have cried to you, O Lord. |
|---|---|
| 2 | Listen to my voice calling to you,
    take notice of my pleas. |
| 3 | Lord, if you counted all our sins against us,
    who could ever stand before you? |
| 4 | But it is in your nature to forgive,
    and it leaves us in awe of you. |
| 5 | I long for the Lord—
    I long from deep within my soul,
    for his word gives me hope. |
| 6 | My soul yearns for the Lord more than those
    who wait anxiously for the morning,
    more than those
    who long for the day to dawn. |
| 7 | Let all in Israel put their hope in the Lord,
    for in the Lord there is mercy,
    and with the Lord grace enough
    to save us all. |
| 8 | The Lord will save the people from all their sins. |

Psalm 131

I am content

1   Lord, I do not aspire to things too far above me,
nor do I worry about great issues.
I do not seek high positions.
Even at heart I do not see myself as great.

2   I have been contented like an infant
snuggling up to its mother
without looking for the breast.
I have been contented like that with God.

3   Wait, O Israel, for the Lord,
now and forever.

Psalm 132

David's line will flourish

1   Lord, remember David—how he suffered,

2   Yet still he made a promise to you, Lord,
the mighty God of Jacob,

3–5   "I will not go home and get into bed,
closing my eyes and falling asleep,
while the Lord, the mighty God of Jacob,
has no place to call home.
I will find such a dwelling place
for the Lord."

6   We heard of this at Ephrathah,
and in the fields of Jaar.

7   We said, "Let us go and worship in your holy place,
bow down before your footstool."

8	Come, O Lord, enter your dwelling place, together with the Ark of your Covenant.
9	May your priests be clothed with righteousness. and your worshippers with joy.
10	For the sake of David your servant do not turn your back on your anointed one.
11	God, you made a solemn promise to David, that his offspring would inherit his throne.
12	If David's children keep the covenant, and the commandments that they are taught, then their children in turn will sit on his throne.
13	For you have chosen to make Zion the place where you will live.
14	You, Lord, declared, "This is the place where I will live contented, for it is the place I have longed for.
15	I will give her people all that they need, and the poor more than enough bread.
16	I will also give her priests salvation as clothing, and her faithful will shout for joy.
17	My desire is that David's line will have strength like the horns of a bull, and will shine out like a bright lamp.
18	While the enemies of David's heirs will be clothed in shame, their crowns will sparkle in splendor."

Psalm 133

In praise of harmony

1   How right and joyous it feels
    when brothers and sisters live together in harmony.

2   It is like the sweet scent of precious perfume filling the air,
    as it is sprinkled on Aaron's head,
    runs down his beard, and onto his robe.

3   It is like the dew settling at night on Hermon,
    and refreshing the mountains around Zion.
    For it is there that the Lord gives his blessing—
    life for evermore.

Psalm 134*

Come, bless the Lord

1   Come all you servants of the lord!
    You who worship together
    through the night
    in the house of God!

2   Lift up your hands in the sanctuary and
    bless the Lord.

3   May the Lord,
    who made both heaven and earth,
    bless you from Zion.

---

* Psalm 134 is the last of the fifteen forming the great Hallel, each of which is also titled *a song of ascents* (see note with Ps 120).

Psalm 135

Praise the Lord who led us from captivity

Praise the Lord! Hallelujah!

1. All you servants of the Lord,
praise the name of the Lord!

2. All you who stand in the house of our Lord,
who gather together
in the courts of the house of our God,

3. Praise the Lord, for he is gracious,
sing praises to his name,
for it is good to do so.

4. He has chosen Jacob and Rachel for himself,
and Israel as his treasure.

5. I know that the Lord is a great God,
A God above all other gods.

6. Whatever the Lord wanted to do he has done,
in the heavens, the earth,
in the seas, and in the depths of the earth.

7. He is the source of the mists that blow in,
and the lightning that accompanies rain.
The wind comes from his storehouse.

8. He is the one who brought death
to the first-born of the Egyptians,
their people and their animals alike.

9. He caused the signs and wonders
in Egypt, affecting Pharoah and his household.

10. The Lord is the one who smashed great nations,
and killed great kings.

11. He ended the reign of Sihon, king of the Amorites,
Og, king of Bashan, and the other kings of Canaan.

12. He gave their lands to the people of Israel,
to the people of Israel as their own.

13	Your name lives forever, O Lord,
	and it will be remembered by each generation.
14	The Lord will pronounce his own people innocent,
	and show compassion to his servants.
15	The other nations have gods who are handmade
	out of silver or gold.
16	They may have mouths, but they do not say a word,
	Eyes, but they see nothing,
17	They have ears that hear not a thing,
	for no breath comes from them.
18	Their gods are made in their own image,
	and they become like each other.
19	Descendants of Israel, bless the Lord!
	Descendants of Aaron, bless the Lord!
20	Descendants of Levi, bless the Lord.
	All you who worship the Lord, bless the Lord.
21	May the Lord of Zion be blessed,
	the Lord who lives in Jerusalem.
	Praise the Lord! Hallelujah!

Psalm 136

A thanksgiving with refrain—God's love will last forever.
It is known to the Jews as "The Great Hallel"

1 O give thanks to the Lord who is so good,
   God's love will last forever.

2 Give thanks to the God of gods,
   God's love will last forever.

3 Give thanks to the Lord of lords
   God's love will last forever.

4   To the only one who does amazing things,
God's love will last forever.

5   To the one who with Wisdom made the heavens,
God's love will last forever.

6   To the one who formed the earth above the waters,
God's love will last forever.

7   Who set the lights of earth in their place,
God's love will last forever.

8   The sun to rule by day,
God's love will last forever.

9   And the moon with the stars by night,
God's love will last forever.

10   Give thanks to the one who brought death to Egypt's first-born,
God's love will last forever.

11   In order to free Israel from their oppression,
God's love will last forever.

12   With great strength in hand and arm,
God's love will last forever.

13   To the one who split the Reed Sea in half,
God's love will last forever.

14   And led Israel through the middle of it,
God's love will last forever.

15   Overwhelming Pharoah and his forces in the waters,
God's love will last forever.

16   Give thanks to the one who led the people
of God through the wilderness,
God's love will last forever.

17   To the one who conquered great kingdoms,
God's love will last forever.

18   And wiped out famous kings,
God's love will last forever.

19   There was Sihon, king of the Amorites,
God's love will last forever.

20	And Og, the king of Bashan, *God's love will last forever.*
21	God gave their land as a heritage, *God's love will last forever.*
22	An inheritance to Israel, the servant of God, *God's love will last forever.*
23	Remembering us when we were at our lowest, *God's love will last forever.*
24	And saving us from our enemies, *God's love will last forever.*
25	God gives food to all who need it, *God's love will last forever.*
26	O give thanks to the God of heaven, *God's love will last forever.*

Psalm 137

Being captives, weeping in Babylon

1	When we sat down on the banks of the rivers in Babylon, we wept, as we remembered Zion.
2	We hung our harps from the poplar trees that grew along the banks.
3	Those who conquered us demanded we be merry. Our captors commanded, "Sing us one of your songs of Zion."
4	How could we possibly sing the Lord's songs in a strange land?
5	If I forget you, O Jerusalem, let my right-hand wither.

6   If I no longer remember you,
    and begin to find my happiness elsewhere,
    let my tongue cleave to the roof of my mouth.

7   Never forget, O Lord, what the children of Edom did
    when Jerusalem was conquered.
    They shouted for it to be razed to the ground.

8   And you, the inhabitants of Babylon—destroyers!
    You will all be destroyed,
    and happy the one who pays you back in the same way
    that you treated us.

9   The Lord will be happy to destroy
    even your tiny babies.

Psalm 138

Praising God with confidence, and asking for God's strength to the end

1   I will praise you with everything I have,
    even in front of other "gods" we worship,
    it is you I praise.

2   I will turn my whole being from self towards you,
    for your compassion and faithfulness
    have magnified your word
    and glorified your name.

3   On the very day I cried to you,
    you answered me.
    You strengthened me with a strength
    that reached into my soul.

4   Every ruler in the world
    will praise you, O Lord,
    when they hear the words you utter.

5   They will sing songs acclaiming you, Lord,
      for great is your glory.

6   Though you, Lord, are so high above me,
      you have respect even for the lowliest,
      while you keep your distance from the proud.

7   If I walk into the thick of trouble,
      you will rescue me—
      you will stretch out your hand to me,
      and lift me far from the enemy's malice.

8   O Lord, whose kindness lasts forever,
      finish the work you have begun in me.
      Do not abandon me now.

Psalm 139

God knows me intimately

1   Lord, you know me, because you have searched me
      through to my inner being.

2   From afar you know my thoughts,
      my ups and downs—
      and you understand them.

3   You know my ins and outs,
      and the way I do things,

4   There is not a word that springs to my tongue
      that you do not already know.

5   You know what is before me and what is behind me,
      for your hand is upon me.

6   Such knowledge is more than I can ever know—
      it is wonderful beyond belief.

7   Is there anywhere I can go to escape your spirit?
      Anywhere I can shake off your presence?

PSALM 139

8   If I could enter heaven I would find you there,
    descend into Sheol, and you would be there too.

9, 10   If I took the wings of the morning
    and flew to earth's furthest bounds,
    you would be there, leading me by the hand.

11 If I thought that darkness would hide me,
    if the light becomes like night around me,

12 Neither darkness nor light will hide me from you—
    both are the same to you.

13 For my very soul belongs to you—
    you wove different parts of me together
    in my mother's womb,

14 It is wonderful and breathtaking—
    the way you made me.
    All your works are amazing, as I know so well.
    It fills me with praise for you.

15, 16 When I was hidden from sight,
    and no-one could see how I was growing,
    you knew the design,
    and the steps in my formation.
    You knew what I would be like
    long before I was born.

17 Your thoughts are precious to me, O God,
    and far too many for me to know.

18 So many that they far outnumber
    the grains of sand on any beach.
    I fall asleep counting them
    and when I wake, I am still at it,
    and you are still with me.

19 You can surely put an end to all the wicked, O God.
    So out of my sight, all you bloodthirsty ones.

20 For you speak words that belittle God,
    and all your actions are against him.

21	I am angered by those who work against you, O God,
	I hate those who hate you.
22	I hate them fully because they work against you,
	and I count them as enemies.
23	Search me, O God, and know my thoughts,
	test me and know my desires.
24	Find out the ways in which I am failing you,
	and put me on the right path—
	the path that endures.

Psalm 140

*Plea to God for safe-keeping from the violent
and to stop the wicked having their way*

1	Rescue me, O God, from evil people.
	Keep me safe from the violent.
2	They dream up crooked schemes,
	and gang together only to fight.
3	Their tongues are as sharp as a snake's—
	their lips full of an adder's venom.
4	O God, keep me out of the hands of evildoers,
	keep me safe from the violent
	who plot my downfall.
5	The arrogant have set traps to catch me,
	they have hidden a net in my path,
	its cords waiting to wrap around me.
6	I turned to the Lord and said,
	You are my God.
	Hear my cry for help.
7	O God, my Lord,
	you are my fortress to shelter me,
	my helmet in battle.

8   Do not let the wicked have their way.
    Do not let their schemes advance at all,
    or else they will puff themselves up even more.

9   May the lies of those who fight me
    turn back on them.

10 Let the burning coals they have prepared for me
    be poured over them.
    Let them fall into their own fire,
    and may that be the end of them.

11 May no evil person become a person of power,
    but rather may evil hunt the evil ones
    and overwhelm them.

12 I know that the Lord will always look after
    the poor and the victimized.

13 Certainly those who live in the right way
    will live in your presence, O God,
    thanking you and praising your name.

Psalm 141*

Prayer to be kept safe from falling into the way of the wicked

1   I cry to you, O Lord.
    Listen to my cries and come quickly.

2   May my prayers come to you
    as an offering to you,
    the lifting of my hands in prayer,
    as incense rising before you.

3   Lord, stand as a guard before my mouth,
    as an examiner at the door of my lips.

---

* The available text of Psalm 141 is very muddled, according to Dahood (p 309). He thinks it could be the prayer of an exile after the fall of Samaria in 721 BC, brought to trial for refusing to participate in the religion of his captors.

4	Let me not be enticed by the wicked to spread false words. Let me not be caught up in their crooked practices, nor partake of their luxuries.
5	Let it be the righteous ones who attack me— it will be a kindness— let them find fault with me— it will be a favor, which will not break me, for my prayer is that I be corrected.
6	Then my words will be heard in judgement of the wrongdoers, and they will be defeated.
7	It may look as though all that we do ends up being scattered around, or being split like wood for the fire.
8	But I put my trust in you, O God. and my eyes follow you. Do not leave me feeling depressed, thinking it was all in vain.
9	Keep me from the traps set by the godless, and from the snares of the evildoers.
10	Let the wicked fall into their own nets, but let me come through safely.

Psalm 142

A cry for help, from someone on their own, who is desperate

1	I voice my requests out loud to the Lord. I cry out to the Lord for mercy.
2	Yes, Lord, I pour out my troubles before you— put into words my complaint.

3   My spirit is laid so low,
    but God, you already know the way I am going,
    and how the enemy have set a snare for me on the path.

4   I look to my right for help—
    no-one who cares about me is to be seen.
    I am helplessly trapped.

5   I turn to you, O Lord,
    crying out that you are my only refuge,
    my only hope in the land of the living.

6   O God, respond to my cry!
    I am feeling desperate.
    Set me free from my persecutors,
    for they are too strong for me.

7   Free me from my prison,
    so that I can praise you freely.
    Deal generously with me
    and let me have good companions
    who circle me round.

Psalm 143

One near death pleads for rescue, not judgement

1   Hear my prayer, O God.
    Listen to my request and,
    in your faithfulness,
    generously answer me.

2   Please do not judge me,
    for no creature alive stands a chance
    of being pronounced innocent before you.

3   Look and see what the enemy has done to me—
    persecuted me and knocked me to the ground,
    and left me in a place so dark
    I might as well be dead.

4   That is why I feel defeated—
utterly desolate.

5   I made an effort, recalling earlier days—
I meditated on what you had done—
I imagined what your hands could still do.

6   I reached out to you,
my soul yearning for your presence,
as a desert longs for water.

7   O Lord, come quickly,
O God, my spirit is fast fading away.
Do not hide from me any longer,
or else I will be with those
who have gone to the place of the departed.

8   Please show me the full extent
of your compassion in the morning,
for I do trust in you.
Show me the way forward,
for I put my life in your hands.

9   Set me free from my enemies—
I flee to you for protection.

10   Teach me to know and do your will,
for you are my Lord.
Lead me again onto level ground
with your spirit of goodness.

11   Restore my life, O Lord,
and lift me out of danger,
in keeping with your nature.

12   In your mercy stop my enemies in their tracks,
destroy those who want to kill my spirit,
and let me be your servant.

Psalm 144

Praising God and asking for safe-keeping and prosperity

1	Blessed are you Lord, my stronghold. You are the one who teaches me to fight, and how to wage war.
2	You are my ruler, my fortress, my deliverer, and my defence— the one I trust, You are the one who subdues people under me.
3	Lord, why do you take into account us humans? What is *Homo sapiens* to you?
4	Human beings must be like a fleeting shadow to you, just a puff of breath.
5	But you are very different, O Lord, for if you opened the heavens and came down to us, you would touch the mountains and they would smoke.
6	You would shoot out lightning as we would arrows, scattering and destroying our enemies.
7, 8	So Lord, lend us your hand from above, for we are in deep waters. Free us from the hand of foreigners, the ones who speak lies and deal in falsehoods.
9	Then I will sing a new song to you, O God, with music on my ten-string harp,
10	Saying that it is you who gives freedom to kings, who saves David, your servant, from destructive violence.
11	Free us from the hands of these foreigners, whose mouths pour out false words, and who deal in deceit.

12 Then our sons will grow up
  like vigorous young saplings,
  and our daughters will stand like stone pillars,
  solid in the foundations of a palace.

13 Our storehouses will be full
  with food of every sort,
  and our ewes will give birth to thousands,
  even ten-thousands of lambs.

14 Then we will have strong working oxen,
  and no-one will have need to break in and steal,
  no-one have any reason to complain.

15 How privileged and joyous
  such a people would be.
  How happy they would be
  with the Lord as their God!

Psalm 145

An acrostic praise song to God the King

1 I will lift you up every day, my God and King,
  and bless your name, O eternal and everlasting one.

2 I will bless you every day,
  and praise your name for ever and ever.

3 You are great indeed, O Lord,
  and deserve great praise!
  Who can even begin to imagine your greatness?

4 Each generation will tell the next what you have done,
  recalling each mighty act.

5 I too will talk about your amazing deeds
  and sing praise-songs of your breath-taking majesty,

6	People will talk of your power and strength,
	and I will recount your awesome deeds one by one.
7	They will remember time and again how good you are,
	how good and how righteous.
8	You, Lord, are full of grace and compassion,
	slow to get angry and quick to show kindness.
9	You are good to everyone,
	and each of your deeds is imbued with mercy.
10	All your actions bring you praise, O Lord.
	All your saints bless you.
11, 12	They tell of the glory of your rule,
	they speak of your power,
	in order to let all people know
	what mighty deeds you have done
	and how glorious is your kingdom.
13	Your kingdom shall last forever—
	it will endure through all generations.
14	You, Lord, lift up any who have fallen,
	and restore the spirit of those who are depressed.
15	Those who keep their eyes focused on you, Lord
	will receive their food in good time,
16	Because you are generous in giving
	every living creature what they need the most.
17	You are just in all you do,
	and faithful through and through.
18	You are close to all those who call on you,
	to those who call on you and mean it.
19	You will fulfil the desires of those who worship you –
	you will hear when they call and save them.
20	You will preserve all those who love you –
	and put an end to the wicked.
21	I will raise my voice in praising you, Lord.
	May all that has life bless your holy name
	for ever and ever.

Psalm 146

Praise the Lord who made everything, and cares for it all

1. Praise the Lord! Halleluyah!
   Praise the Lord, O my soul!

2. I will sing praises to God as long as I have breath.
   I will praise God my whole life long.

3. Do not put your trust in ordinary people,
   not even in nobility,
   for they cannot help.

4. Their life can be cut short,
   and their plans come to nothing.

5. You will be glad that you trusted in God—
   that the God of Jacob and Rachel is there to help you.

6. Our God who made the heavens,
   the earth, the seas, and all that exists,
   is forever trustworthy.

7. Our God ensures the oppressed find justice,
   gives the hungry food,
   and sets the prisoner free.

8. The Lord, who loves those who do right,
   gives sight to the blind,
   and hope to the depressed.

9. The Lord looks after any stranger,
   aids the orphan and the widow,
   but turns the way of the wicked upside down.

10. The Lord will reign forever.
    Our Lord, the God of Zion,
    will reign through every generation.
    Praise the Lord! Halleluyah!

Psalm 147

*Praise the Lord who controls the stars and the seasons,
and is rebuilding Jerusalem*

1	Halleluyah! Praise the Lord, all of you! It is so good to praise our Lord, and such a pleasure to do so.
2	The Lord is rebuilding Jerusalem, gathering in the scattered Israelites.
3	He heals those who are broken in spirit, binding up the places where they hurt the most.
4, 5	Our Lord is so great in power and understanding, that he knows how many stars there are and the name of each one.
6	The Lord takes care of the lowly, but has no time for the wicked.
7	Sing your thanks to our Lord— sing songs with the harp.
8	Sing about God who spreads clouds across the skies, gathering rain for the earth, making the grass grow on the hills.
9	He provides food for the cattle, with enough left over for the ravens.
10	God does not find his pleasure in the speed of a horse, nor the speed of a person, for that matter.
11	He finds pleasure in those who worship him— in those who find hope in his mercy.
12	Praise the Lord, all in Jerusalem. Praise him all in Zion.
13	God has given you strong bars across your gates, and strong children growing within.

14	He has given you peace along your borders,
	and a bountiful supply of grain.
15	God proclaims his word over the earth.
	Like thunder it spreads abroad.
16	Then the snow falls like wool,
	and frost descends like ash.
17	He scatters hail like breadcrumbs.
	His cold—who can stand it?
18	Just as quickly, at his word, they melt.
	As his breath warms the wind
	the ice turns to water.
19	He has given his word to Jacob's people,
	his laws and justice to Israel.
20	He has not done this to any other nation—
	they know nothing about his laws.
	Halleluyah!
	Praise the Lord! All of you.

Psalm 148

Praise the lord, all of earth and heaven and all its creatures

1	Praise the Lord, from the heavens!
	Praise the Lord from the highest points!
2	Praise the Lord, all his messengers.
	Praise him all his attendants.
3	Praise him, sun and moon.
	Praise him, all stars that glow with light.
4	Praise him, planets and our Milky Way,
	other universes and the space beyond.
5, 6	Let them all praise the name of the Lord—
	he alone commanded and they were created

and put into place,
where, by his decree they will exist for ever.

7 Praise the Lord, all the earth,
from its very depths, where fire belches out,
to its heights, covered in mist.

8 Praise him snow, hail and lashing winds,
carrying out his word.

9 Praise the Lord, all mountains, and hills,
all trees, from cedars to fruit-trees,

10 All wild creatures, and all tame,
all creatures that creep and those that fly.

11 Praise him, all people on earth,
including kings, princes and leaders,

12 From young men and women
to old men and children,

13 May they all praise the Lord,
whose very name is wonderful,
his glory above and beyond
everything that exists.

14 He will take the praise of his people
and raise it to new heights,
giving them strength
and keeping them close to him.
Halleluyah! Praise the Lord!

Psalm 149

*Praise to God by a nation victorious in battle,
ending with a wish for vengeance*

1. Halleluyah! Praise the Lord!
   Come and sing a new song to the Lord,
   all of us praising him together.

2. Let the children of Israel find joy in God their creator,
   the children of Zion in God their King.

3. With music and dance, let them come together
   to praise his name.

4. The Lord is delighted when his people do this,
   and he gives victory to the humble.

5. May the joy of praising God follow them home,
   so that even in bed they are praising him.

6. Let the praise of God be always on their lips,
   but let them keep their weapons at the ready,

7. To inflict vengeance on the nations
   who act against God.

8. Binding them with chains,
   even their kings and nobles.

9. Let them pronounce on these
   the judgement written against them.
   This would be an honor to all God's faithful.
   Halleluyah! Praise the Lord!
   All of you!

Psalm 150

A call for everyone to praise God with full orchestra and with dance

1 Halleluyah! Praise the Lord! All of you!
   Praise God in the house of worship,
   praise God wherever you are.

2 Praise the Lord who is the greatest,
   and who does great deeds of power.

3–5 Praise the Lord to the accompaniment
   of stringed instruments—
   Praise God with lyre, harp and flute.
   Blow the trumpet.
   Clash the cymbals.
   Shake the tambourines.
   Dance your praise.

6 May everything that has breath
   Praise the Lord!
   Halleluyah!

Glossary

Acrostic psalm – the lines of the psalm begin with successive letters of the Hebrew alphabet, although the alphabet is often not complete. Ps 11, Ps 25, Ps 119.

Baal-Peor or Baal of Peor – Ps 106:28. The Israelites had an idolatrous relationship with the god of Peor, which is probably in the trans-Jordan hills. (Deut 4:3.)

Baca – Ps 84:6. unidentified valley. It's meaning is associated with weeping.

Bashan – Ps 22:12, 68:15. a fertile plateau across south Syria, with mountains, forests, cattle, sheep. Their king of renown was Og,(Deut 1:4, Neh 9:22, Ps 135:11, 136:20.)

Cherubim – Ps 18:10, Ps 80:1. a celestial being. There are several types associated with the word. The only thing they have in common is that they are winged. They are strong, pull God's chariot, or act as his steed.

Dassie – Ps 104:18. a small rock mammal found in South Africa, also translated as the rock hyrax or the coney.

Edom, Ishmaelites, Moab, Hagarites – and others named in Ps 83:6 – 8, all traditional enemies of Israel, situated to the south and east.

Ephraim and Mannasseh – Ps 60:7. two tribes of Israel named for Joseph's two sons. They were important in the Northern Kingdom, Israel, with Shiloh, its early capital.

Gilead – Ps 60:7, Jer 8:22, region in the trans-Jordan between Bashan and Moab. There was a balm produced in Gilead, but no-one knows its composition.

God Almighty – translates God Sabaoth, i.e. God of Hosts, a military term.

God above all – in place of God Most High

Glossary

God's Name – Personal names for the Hebrews were very important because they revealed the character and identity of a person. If one knew the name, one could know the person. Hence the importance of the name of God. In Hebrew it was YHWH, written in English as Yahweh. (at one time mistakenly translated as Jehovah) It was so revered that it came to be no longer voiced, until no-one knew how it was pronounced. It is translated as Lord. Other names were used in place of the most sacred name:

Yahweh Sabaoth: Lord of Hosts, commander of armies, translated now as Lord Almighty.

Elohim and *'El*, a generic name for a god, both translated as God.

Adonai often used as a substitute for YHWH, my great Lord.

El Elyon literally God Most High, from the Canaanite.

El Elohim - the God of gods

Hallel – a Hebrew word meaning praise . Hallelujah = Hallel u Yah = praise Yah = Praise the Lord. Found only in the psalms and then only in Ps 104 – 150.

Hebrew – The language of the ancient Israelites, and the language in which the psalms were written. It has twenty-three letters, giving acrostic psalms that number of verses, which is not always the case. No original manuscript of the psalms exists and often the oldest available are difficult to decipher.

Hesed – a frequently used Hebrew word, an attribute of God, for which there is no exact equivalent in English. In the KJV (King James Version) it was translated as "lovingkindness", and in the NRSV (New Revised Standard Version) as "steadfast love". I have used various words to convey its breadth of meaning – *constant love, compassion, kindness, mercy,* among them. e.g. Ps 26;3, 33:5, 22, 36:5, 7, 10, 103:4.

Hermon – Ps 42:6, the highest mountain in the region, towering over the Bashan plateau and the upper Jordan valley.

Horn – Ps 18:2, 75:5,10, apart from the usual meaning, the symbolic meaning is that horns showed the strength of a person, e.g, Ps 75:5, "do not lift up your horn on high" means "do not boast of your power." Ps 75:10, "I will cut off all the horns of the wicked" means "I will cut down the strength of the wicked."

Glossary

Israel – collective name for the Northern Kingdom as distinct from Judah.

Israel, Jacob, Joseph, Judah – etc, or the children of Israel, etc…The tribes formed by the descendants of Jacob, and the others. The descendants of Jacob, whose name was changed by God to Israel, (Gen 32:28, Gen 35:10) were also known as Israel, or the Israelites.

Kedar – Ps 120:5, a land far from Israel towards the Arabian desert.

Leviathan – Ps 74:13,14 A primeval sea monster who battles against the good gods of the ancient world and is ultimately defeated. He also became the monster whom the God of Israel defeated. Often in recent translation a *whale*.

Mannasseh - see **Ephraim**

Mizar – Ps 42;6, unknown small hill, probably near Mt Hermon.

Meribah – Ex 17:7, Ps 95:8, the same as Massah – according to tradition the spring in the wilderness where Israel tested the Lord. The word means testing or trial.

Meshech – Ps 120:5, a nation in the east near Syria.

Musical instruments – Ps 92:3, 137:2, 98;5,6, 150:3 – 5, There were a variety of musical instruments, some we know, the ram's horn or shophar, being the most ancient, the trumpet made of metal, and the harp or lyre, a hand-held stringed instrument. There was also the tambourine. Others we do not know. I did not substitute modern instruments.

Name – a personal name was very important because it revealed who the person was. To know it signified a relationship with the person. A name could be used symbolically, and it could stand for the person themselves – the same for God. Some examples: Ps 33:21, trust in his holy name, Ps 83:17, that they may seek your name.

Negeb – Ps 126:4, the southern dry area of Judah

Psalm – the word originally meant a song. The word is from the Greek *psalmos*, which translated the Hebrew word *mizmor*, a song. The psalms consist of prayers, thanksgiving, teaching poems, praise-poems, and songs, originally written in Hebrew. Some of them stretch back to the beginnings of recorded history in the Israelite nation.

Glossary

Psalter – a book of Psalms. The name originates in the Greek word, *psalterion*, a stringed instrument.

Rahab – **1.** Ps 89:10, refers to a mythical creature with which God did battle, in order to create the world. **2.** Ps 87:4, a pejorative name for Egypt.

Red Sea or Reed Sea – Ps 106:9, 22, the word translated as *red* is literally *reed*, so it should be the *Reed Sea*. There is no agreement as to where it was, with three main possibilities on the route the Israelites may have taken.

Righteous and Sinner – The "righteous" in the Psalms continually do battle with the "sinner" or the "wicked".

Today we seldom talk about "sinners", "the wicked", or "the righteous" as in the past. Both the words, but also the concepts they express, are no longer accepted as they were. We now tend to substitute milder words or phrases. These are still fundamental concepts in the Psalms. I used for

> Righteous—just, right-doing, upright Ps 14:5, Ps 18:20
> Sinner—unjust, wrong-doing, crooked Ps 51;5,
> The wicked—a phrase such as "those who do wrong" Ps 15:4, Ps 17:9

Sacrifices and burnt-offerings – Ps 40:6, Ps 51:16, Ps 69:31, Where the Hebrew people were referred to, I partly kept the original concepts, but in Ps 50:14, Ps 54:6, Ps 51:17, Ps 66:13 – 15, when they applied to an individual I substituted what is more applicable today.

Salem – see Jerusalem

Salvation – Ps 7:10, 27;1,60:5, 86:2,106;21 being saved or a savior. In the psalms this has more of an everyday meaning, i.e. creating, enlarging or broadening the space within a community for life to flourish. This is usually with divine help.

It can also mean that God rescues and delivers the individual or nation from a situation of opposition and peril to one of spaciousness, prosperity, and well-being. Other terms are used like redemption, ransom, pardon, rescue.

Sheba and Seba – Ps 72:10, 15, distant wealthy countries.

Shechem, Succoth Valley, Moab – and other places in Ps 60:6 – 9 and Ps 108:7 – 14. They are all countries near to Israel. The ones in vs 6 and 7 are

Glossary

Israelite territories and belong to God. The ones in vs 8 and 9 are traditional enemy countries, but God is in control of them as well.

Sheol – Ps 9:17, 88:5, the Hebrew underworld, abode of the dead. It is a gloomy place where the departed go but is not fiery like Hades or hell. It was also the place of the waters of chaos. To be in Sheol is to be forgotten and inactive.

Sinner – see Righteous and Sinners

Soul – Ps 33:20, 21, Ps 49:15, 142:4, It has a wide range of meanings, including a person, (a living soul) or a life force. At first for a Hebrew, souls were persons, but later the Greek idea of a body as the vehicle of the soul was adopted, with its duality.

Tarshish – Ps 48:7, Ps 72:10, 15, an unknown seaport, usually associated with Jonah.

Torah – Ps 119, Law of the Jewish people. It has a wide meaning, incorporating instruction towards a way of organising society in a just, equitable, and non-corruptible manner. God was seen as the originator of the rules, commandments, or code of conduct, that grew out of this intention. Psalm 119 is the key psalm on God's instruction or law.

Worldview of the Biblical Israelite – Ps 65:9, 99:1, 102:25, 104:5, 115:3, the Biblical world was a three-tiered world, with the nether-world, called "Sheol" under the earth, the earth a layer on top of that and, forming a massive dome over it all, the heavens (it was plural in Hebrew). The heavens were full of water and all weather originated there. It was the place of the stars, the sun and moon. The dome of heaven was held up by the pillars of the earth. It was also the place where God lived. From here God directly controlled everything. He is depicted coming to earth in storms, Ps 77:18, 19, Ps 18:11–14.

Zion and Jerusalem – II Sam 5:6-10 tells us that David and his men took Jerusalem from the Jebusites. From this passage it is also apparent that Jerusalem, Zion, and the City of David are one and the same. King David then made it his capital city. Salem is another word used for Jerusalem.

Zoan – Ps 78:12, 43, the residence of the kings of Egypt during the tenth to seventh centuries BCE, the ruins now about 120 km NE of Cairo. Referred to in Num 13:22. A different place to Zoar. (Gen 14: 1-12)

Glossary

BIBLIOGRAPHY

Alter, Robert. *The Book of Psalms: A Translation with Commentary.* New York: Norton, 2007.
Bell, John L. *Living with the Psalms.* London: SPCK, 2021.
Bonhoeffer, Dietrich. *Prayerbook of the Bible: An Introduction to the Psalms.* Translated from the German by James Burtness. Minneapolis: Fortress, 1996.
Brueggemann, Walter. *Israel's Praise: Doxology against Idolatry and Ideology.* Philadelphia: Fortress, 1988.
Cotter, Jim. *Psalms for a Pilgrim People.* 3 vols. Harrisburg, PA: Morehouse, 1989–93.
Dahood, Mitchell, SJ. *The Anchor Bible, Book of Psalms, Introduction, Translation and Notes:* Garden City, New York: Doubleday and Co, 1968.
The Grail. *The Psalms: A New Translation,* London: Collins Fontana Books, 1963.
Harper's Bible Dictionary: Achtemeier, Paul J, General Editor. San Francisco: Harper and Row, 1985.
Julian of Norwich, *Showings,* translated with an introduction by Edmund Colledge and James Walsh, Classics of Western Spirituality: New York, Paulist, 1978.
Merrill, Nan C. *Psalms for Praying: An Invitation to Wholeness*: New York: Continuum, 1998.
The New Interpreter's Bible, *Volume 4, Psalms*: Nashville: Abingdon, 1996.
Peterson, Eugene H. *The Message: New Testament, with Psalms and Proverbs:* Colorado Springs, NavPress, 1996.
Seerveld, Calvin. *Voicing God's Psalms:* Grand Rapids, Michigan: William B Eerdmans, 2005.
Westermann, Claus. *The Living Psalms:* translated from the German by JR Porter, Grand Rapids, Michigan: William B Eerdmans, 1984.

TRANSLATIONS OF THE BIBLE

King James Authorized Version, 1611

New Revised Standard Version, 1989

New International Version, Psalms, 1978

Revised English Bible, 1989

www.ingramcontent.com/pod-product-compliance
Lightning Source LLC
Chambersburg PA
CBHW071430150426
43191CB00008B/1098